THE 1924 TORNADO IN LORAIN & SANDUSKY

THE 1924 TORNADO IN LORAIN & SANDUSKY

DEADLIEST IN OHIO HISTORY

BETSY D'ANNIBALE

THE History PRESS

Published by The History Press
Charleston, SC 29403
www.historypress.net

First published 2014

Manufactured in the United States

ISBN 978.1.62619.636.0

Library of Congress CIP data applied for.

Notice: The information in this book is true and complete to the best of our knowledge. It is offered without guarantee on the part of the author or The History Press. The author and The History Press disclaim all liability in connection with the use of this book.

This book is dedicated to the to the victims of the June 28, 1924 Lorain/ Sandusky Tornado, and to their families and descendants, as well as to the indomitable spirit of the people living in the shoreline communities of Lake Erie.

CONTENTS

PREFACE

The seeds for *The 1924 Tornado in Lorain and Sandusky: Deadliest in Ohio History* were sown when I was just a child growing up in Elyria, Ohio, a city less than ten miles from Lorain. In the late 1950s and early '60s, most Ohio families from that area and era would jam into their family cars and drive to the beach for picnics every summer.

In those days, there were still miles of farmland between Elyria and Lorain. Farmland meant endless fields of corn and farms stands selling vegetables and fruit. Driving along the country roads, listening to the adults chatting, I would impatiently wait to get to our destination. Those ten miles in a hot, crowded car seemed endlessly long to a child of six.

But then my uncle's old Ford would suddenly turn a corner, and there we were—dead ahead was water as far as the eye could see.

People who talk about small, peaceful lakes have no idea what it is like to experience one of the Great Lakes. Actually, "confront" is a better word—one views a tranquil mountain lake, but one confronts the Great Lakes. Together and individually, they are forces to be reckoned with.

Even on a calm, balmy day, there is nothing peaceful about Lake Erie. You know instinctively that the lake demands respect. It was, and still is, a presence, a tangible force in itself, with its own historical memories.

Memories filled with secrets.

Carved by glaciers, nameless for millennia, called Lac du Chat and now known as Erie, the names change but the lake doesn't. When I would peer out at the endless water, I always felt something was looking back at me. Of course, I was just a child—and an imaginative one, too—so no one paid any attention.

But if I was entranced with Lake Erie, I was also curious about the houses nearby, and this wasn't fanciful but practical. I would study the structures and how they suddenly looked different along the shore. It just didn't seem right to me. When I would question this, I'd get vague answers. With the persistence of a child, I kept probing until, finally, someone told me about the tornado that came off the lake and hit Lorain and Sandusky. This was whispered because no one wanted to upset my grandmother.

What I discovered were the seeds of this story.

Helen Valassis was haunted by memories of the tornado that struck in 1924.

I discovered that my grandfather and grandmother, horrified by the terrible stories starting to trickle into Elyria (the *Chronicle Telegram* was the first paper to report about the tornado), had made the trek to Lorain on the night of the storm to see if Mary Peters, my grandfather's sister, survived.

They set off on the Elyria Lorain trolley until the line halted because of downed trees and wires and walked the rest of the way into the city before the National Guard arrived and set up a curfew. They saw the wreckage of cars bobbing out on the waves and the empty, gaping holes where proud houses had once stood.

They walked, along with the homeless and injured, down dark, debris-filled streets, lit only by lanterns, searching for Fourth Street. People moved around them, weeping in pain and shock. The experience of seeing the destruction of the storm, the shattered houses and dead bodies and hearing the moans of the injured left a profound effect on my grandmother. Eventually, they found Mary Peters, my great-aunt, alive, along with her husband and children, safe and sound. My grandmother developed a phobia of storms. To the day she died at ninety-six in Elyria, Ohio, she would head for the basement when a dark cloud appeared. In many ways, she was a victim of the tornado, as, I'm sure, are many other people who went unrecorded.

This account is really the compilation of the stories of the victims of the storm. Unfortunately, I could not tell everyone's story. Some victims, such as Edward Wittenback, were listed as dying in two different places. His name was also spelled Wyttenbach in some accounts. Edward is listed in some records as dying at Lakeview Beach, but other records list him as killed at the Crystal Restaurant.

There were also discrepancies in the spelling of last names and ages. In the 1924 list of victims, there is a Harold Lewenstein, age twenty-eight, who died at Lakeview Beach. Also listed was a Harold Lawenstein, age seven, who died at the same beach. Were they father and son? Was Harold listed incorrectly? This is a matter for future historians to discover. In the confusion of the rescues, information was occasionally incorrect.

I selected a few of the victims and survivors who seemed representative and whose histories were fairly well documented. This is why I chose Ellen Meredith and Harry Buttle, siblings and victims of the bathhouse collapse, and Bessie Widzer, who died at the State Theater. The Foisy family and Mary Peters were immigrants who were seeking a better life in a foreign land. Mary Peters and her husband, John, discussed their experiences with my own family members, so their memories were easily documented. Gertrude Mills owned a prosperous business. Dorothy LaLonde and Mary Campbell died at the Crystal Restaurant.

Mary Kodelja was one of the first to die, and her history is so poignant that I felt compelled, as a writer, to document her existence. The fact that we have her photograph preserved on her tombstone was especially moving to me. She had a brief life, but now, perhaps, a more famous one.

I followed the same logic when I picked the Van Deusen family. They were an established family living in a solid home, and the adults were knowledgeable about surviving a storm. They did everything right in heading for shelter in the basement. One would have picked them to survive, and yet, tragedy struck them five times.

The very capriciousness of the tornado in selecting its victims was a thread that kept reappearing as I researched this book. I found many stories of people who were killed, their mangled, crushed bodies physically touching someone who lived and, perhaps, was almost unscathed. Wilbur Van Deusen died in his aunt's arms while she suffered only minor injuries.

Gertrude Mills's death was most poignant in this regard. It took over a day to reach her crushed body, yet the chicks in the crate nearby were unhurt. It was the chirping of the little birds that alerted rescuers to life still existing in what was the wasteland of the Mills Feed Store.

It is so hard to predict in a tornado who will live and who will die. I think this is the essence of the physical force of the twister; it has an impulsive, uncanny way of moving along a path of destruction that can change in the blink of an eye; an almost drone-like essence in that it selects its path and its victims, and a man can only pray that he will not be a victim. That very unpredictability is what holds our fascination.

To be forewarned of the imminent arrival of a storm is perhaps the only chance people have. This should give us pause and make us consider our options in the face of future super storms.

In closing, I must say that the victims of the 1924 tornado were a brave, interesting group of people. I have sincerely come to admire them and almost feel I know them. To record their last day on earth was an honor, and it is with pride that I write this memorial to their passing.

ACKNOWLEDGEMENTS

With acknowledgements and sincere thanks to Nan Card at the Rutherford B. Hayes Presidential Center; Janice Tallman at the Ohio Historical Society; Ron Davidson at the Sandusky Library Archives Research Center; Joanne Cornelius and Vern Morrison at the Michael Schwartz Library at Cleveland State University; Robert T. Smith and Andrew Allan for their invaluable assistance with the photographs; Valerie Smith at the Lorain Public Library for her assistance with photographs and historical details; Executive Director Barbara Piscopo and the staff at the Lorain Historical Society for allowing me to peruse their records; the Elyria Public Library historical records and librarians; and to Carolyn Sipkovsky, Sue and Mark Antolik, Mary Jane Febonio and Thomas Valassis for their reminiscences of family members who went through the tornado of 1924, as well as the citizens of Lorain and Sandusky for their gracious hospitality.

I also wish to thank Steve Finch for asking so many insightful questions about this work, forcing me to reconsider editing changes that would make the story more understandable to my readers; my son Paul D'Annibale, who advised me on geological issues in the formation of the Great Lakes; my son John Christopher D'Annibale for never doubting I would finish this project, proofing the manuscript and offering valuable advice on the historical presentation; my husband, John Carl D'Annibale, for his patience in listening to my tales of woe, encouraging and supporting my efforts and listening for countless hours to the stories I unearthed as I researched this book; and the supportive and creative staff at The History Press—especially my editor, Greg Dumais—who have made this effort a joy to complete.

Thank you one and all!

INTRODUCTION

The living owe it to those who can no longer speak to tell their story for them.
—Czeslaw Mitosz, The Issa Valley: A Novel

It was a steamy day in June, almost ninety years ago, when a young lifeguard stood watch atop the lifeguard station at Lakeview Park beach on Lake Erie and scanned the horizon. High up in his stand, he could see there was a storm brewing out on the lake, but it caused little concern among the hundreds of bathers who were finding relief from the extremely hot and muggy day. If anything, they were enjoying the increasingly high waves beginning to pound the sand. Below his chair, children began to squeal with laughter as they played in the rough surf.

But the lifeguard took his summer job seriously, and he kept close watch. His vigilance made him the first person to see the black funnel slowly start to descend from the underbelly of the offshore storm. He recognized what it was immediately—a tornado, and it was coming straight for the beach.

The lifeguard picked up his megaphone and began to shout out warnings. He then leaped from his chair and ran up and down the beach, but over the crash of the waves and the happy laughter of the bathers, it took a few minutes to alert the crowd. At last, people began to listen to him and shift their eyes toward the angry lake. As they realized the danger, they leaped up and ran for shelter, but the funnel was charging toward them at almost one hundred miles per hour, too fast for many people to make it to safety.

It hit the beach with one-hundred-mile-per-hour winds and suction power capable of lifting a building with impunity.

It was no longer a question of reaching shelter. Now, it was only a matter of luck and grace that would determine who would live and who would die.

The F4 tornado had formed over Sandusky Bay, twenty-six miles to the west, a half hour earlier. It struck Sandusky, Ohio, and then shifted back onto the water, racing directly east. Then, as if following a map, it abruptly changed course again, turned south and made a direct hit on Lorain, Ohio. Its landfall was the crowded beach at Lakeview Park. In just over five minutes, the black, swirling, killer wind would level a city and slip into the record books of deadly disasters and crushed, ruined lives.

Our modern world is one of legendary super storms; Katrina, Hugo and Sandy are famous hurricanes. The tornadoes that have hit the Midwest and southern parts of the United States are legendary. The names of these killers have become famous, usually taking on the monikers of the communities they destroyed or the days they occurred. Hence, we have the Xenia, Ohio Tornado and the Palm Sunday Tornado. When they struck the United States, their deadly paths were avidly followed by millions of people on television and radio. Now, with Facebook, Twitter and cellphone technology that make instant communication available, new storms are discussed as they are happening.

Factoring in our own safety, what else has caused our fascination with extreme weather? Perhaps it began with the deluge of reports on global warming and the accompanying weather changes that would ensue. These changes could possibly energize more violent storms. This interest in weather is fueled by twenty-four-hour-a-day, seven-day-a-week weather coverage on television. The modern viewer is "on the spot" at whatever super storm calamity is devastating some portion of our world.

Then, with the landfall of Hurricane Katrina, Americans had to face the vulnerability of our coastal cities. Perhaps this heightened sense of awareness perversely makes us feel more confident in the face of danger. We've bought our extra batteries, stocked up on water, bought nonperishable food and filled the gas tank. Now we are safe.

But the truth is quite different.

Ninety years have come and gone, but if we are honest, humanity is still at the mercy of the weather. Hurricanes, tornadoes, blizzards, floods and drought are weather-related events we delude ourselves into believing we have tamed.

Our only real achievement is our ability to occasionally predict what will happen, giving us a slight edge before disaster strikes. Make no mistake, preparation and evacuation plans in danger areas are powerful tools to keep us safe, and we are lucky we have this knowledge today. People on the East Coast of the United States had days to make evacuation plans when Hurricane Sandy was moving north toward New York City and the Jersey Shore.

But what if we never knew these storms were coming? What if we lolled around on a summer day, oblivious to danger, and suddenly, like the hammer of Thor descending on mankind, we were hit? This is what happened one summer day in northern Ohio when two weather systems, one high and one low, collided over Lake Erie and spawned a killer tornado.

For the citizens of Sandusky and Lorain, Ohio, on that beautiful, sultry summer day in June, there was no early warning system, no hint of the cyclonic monster twisting into existence on Sandusky Bay, creating a force of destruction. Forged in lightning and hurricane-strength winds, the F4 tornado blasted into their communities and, in just minutes, irrevocably changed their lives forever.

The morning of June 28, 1924, began for most people with eager anticipation of a fun-filled weekend. Saturday was a half day of work for factory personnel, and Sunday was a holiday for everyone. The blue, warm waters of Lake Erie beckoned to swimmers, boaters and those who just wanted to sprawl in the sun and picnic.

It ended in shocking destruction and death.

This is the story of quixotic twists of fate; the tornado spared one man yet crushed another, sucked one woman into the sky, never to be seen again, and barely touched a friend standing close by. It was a capricious demon that plunged innocent children into a smashed theater basement, rained down four stories of debris from the apartments above them and then let one child survive uninjured while a friend, only six inches away, was crushed to death in seconds.

What happened ninety years ago in northern Ohio, when the sunny blue sky morphed into a macabre black and green firmament, was a cataclysm forged by many special factors. It is a story of location, population and, ultimately, survival.

Every storm is different, and every community caught in the path of a black twister stands alone. In this way, the June 28, 1924 Sandusky/Lorain tornado was a unique event. This F4 tornado was not born on the great, flat plains of Oklahoma or Kansas. The areas leveled were not the corn and wheat fields of Missouri or Iowa farmed by the grandchildren of covered wagon pioneers.

This tornado was a child of Lake Erie, first forming as a waterspout before exploding into a massive wind funnel. Then it slammed into the shipyards, railroads and factories of northern Ohio and destroyed the homes of those who worked in those industries. The brunt of the storm was born by the immigrants from war-torn Europe who came to America to work in the steel mills and shipyards of northern Ohio.

In 1920, the population of Lorain was 37,295 people, of whom 11,927 were foreign born. Unlike the earlier settlers from Germany, the British Isles and northern Europe, the new immigrants came from central and southern Europe.

Their embarkation points are reflected in the clubs and churches they founded in their new home. In 1903, the Transylvania Saxon Society was established, followed, in 1906, by the Bohemian Women's Lodge. In 1907, the Romanian Beneficiary and Cultural Society was formed, to be closely followed by the Czechoslovakians, who built their Sokol Hall in 1908. In 1913, Saints Peter and Paul Russian Greek Orthodox Church opened its doors, and in 1914, a Hungarian-language newspaper, *Lorain es Videke*, was started to assist the Hungarian population. The development of these ethnic enclaves continued right up to 1923, when the American Croatian Club was opened.

These immigrant groups—Poles, Czechs, Germans, French, Greek, Italians, Jews, Ukrainians and Hungarians, to name a few—came from tough and hardy stock. They came to work and to carve out a better world. When adversity struck, as it did on June 28, 1924, they were momentarily stunned.

But they were not defeated.

To relate this story, you have to write about the people, the communities and the history of the lake on which they lived. The restoration of these cities after June 24, 1928, is a testament to their spirit and determination.

INTRODUCTION

Just the word "tornado" inspires curiosity and fear in most people—and with good reason. In the hierarchy of weather systems, tornadoes stand right next to hurricanes, floods and heat waves as the most deadly weather events on earth. The devastation from a tornado is equal to that of a major earthquake or volcanic eruption, both geological events.

The word "tornado" derives initially from the Latin word for thunder and then from the Spanish word *tornear*, "to twist." It is an apt description. Tornadoes usually herald their approach with deafening thunder, hail and wild, twisting winds. Then the funnel itself descends from the black mass of racing clouds and begins to assault the earth below. In our common lexicon, "moved like a tornado" or "looked like a tornado hit it" immediately bring to mind intense speed, accompanied by chaos and destruction.

Tornadoes are called many different things. Twisters, cyclones, steam devils, gustanados and dust devils are only a few of the names. Over water, they have been called waterspouts, frequent occurrences on Lake Erie.

Writers have incorporated tornadoes into the plot lines of movies and literature. L. Frank Baum wrote *The Wizard of Oz* about a girl named Dorothy who is swept up by a tornado. In 1939, the book was made into a move starring Judy Garland. *Twister*, starring Helen Hunt and Bill Paxton, was a hit in 1996. The movie recounted the adventures of a group of storm chasers.

Tornadoes are found everywhere on earth, having been noted on every continent except Antarctica, but they are mainly considered an American phenomenon. Over 75 percent of all tornadoes each year are on the American mainland.

So what, exactly, is a tornado?

The definition of a tornado is simple: it is a rotating column of air that maintains contact with both the surface of the earth—whether land or water—and the storm clouds above it. This whirlwind is created when a low and a high weather system collide, usually forming a thunderstorm. A thunderstorm that rotates is called a super cell.

Within the funnel of the tornado, the winds rotate at killer speeds, often reaching three hundred miles per hour, and in some huge tornadoes, speeds have been recorded at five hundred miles per hour. These huge funnels, rotating upward, create vacuums that literally suck up anything in their paths. Once inside the funnel, an object is pulverized by the power of the wind-swirling debris.

In the Northern Hemisphere, tornadoes rotate counterclockwise. In the Southern Hemisphere, they move clockwise. Half of all tornadoes found in the United States each year are primarily in the Midwest, an area unscientifically dubbed "Tornado Alley." The United States has about eight hundred to one thousand tornadoes annually, but most are weak and do little damage.

The United States' weather spawns so many tornadoes because of the topography of the country. First, the Rocky Mountains run north–south, not east–west, and second, the Gulf of Mexico is a major source of hot, humid air. With the Rockies creating a basin of sorts in the Midwest, the warm Gulf air doesn't disperse east–west, but flows north, where the high system often collides with low, cold-weather systems, triggering major thunderstorms

As violent as they are, tornadoes are very finicky about developing. Even today, scientists are still not sure why some super cell thunderstorms produce funnels and others don't. They do know that weather conditions must be just so. A collision of a warm air front with a cold one is necessary, creating a thunderstorm with strong winds. Weather conditions are best in late spring and early summer. Most tornadoes are formed in May, followed by June, April and July.

Time of day is important, too. The greatest numbers of tornadoes break out between four and five o'clock in the afternoon, when the heating of the earth by the sun is most intense. It is interesting to note that the deadly tornado that hit Lorain and Sandusky was textbook perfect in that it hit on June 28 right around the five o'clock hour on a hot, muggy summer day.

People who have lived through tornadoes and survived have reported the noise of the approaching twister as similar to the sound of a freight train moving overhead or the blast of loud cannons. Another common observation is the color of the sky before the storm actually arrives. People speak of a "tornado sky," which is described as yellow and green, slowly turning to black, with flashes of giant lightning bolts.

Tornadoes cause damage in several ways. The low pressure inside the funnel creates a suction effect. As the tornado moves overhead, it literally sucks up everything in its path, and as it moves on and the pressure changes, objects are flung far and wide. Each year, the damage to property from twisters ranges from the hundreds of millions of dollars to over $1 billion annually.

Another destructive development in the creation of a tornado is the dust and debris field that grows as it moves along its path. Objects in the path of the funnel can be sucked up or pulverized by the external debris caused by the violent wind.

Tornadoes vary in size. Some are relatively small, barely a few yards across, while the most destructive can be over a mile long. Their paths are unpredictable, and it has been noted that sometimes a tornado will move down one side of a street, mowing down every building in its path, while the other side of the street is left standing. Occasionally, a large tornado will suddenly split into two or three funnels, increasing the damage and unpredictability of the storm. Some storms have reportedly spawned over a dozen small funnels at their peak activity.

One of the common causes of death and destruction during a tornado is the ability of the funnel to grasp huge objects; carry them along in a deadly, spiraling whirlwind; and then toss the objects out from high in the air. Cars, trucks, parts of buildings and, sadly, human and animal remains are often found far from their original locations. Occasionally, someone or something will be picked up by the funnel, carried away and set down without any damage, but this is rare. It is safe to say that if you are sucked up by a tornado, it probably is the end of the road for you.

The Fujita Scale rates tornadoes by the amount of damage they cause. Through Doppler radar, meteorologists make predictions of the power of oncoming storms, but after the tornadoes pass, scientists must examine the damage and determine the Fujita level of the storms. A level one can uproot trees, but a level five is capable of destroying a city. The tornado that passed through Xenia, Ohio, in 1975 destroyed half the city. The vacuum sucking power of the funnel was so great that it was reported the twister pulled caskets out of fresh graves.

Today, with Doppler radar at the disposal of meteorologists, approaching tornadoes are usually spotted in time for a warning to go out over television and radio, and now this information will go to Smartphones if a person has installed a weather-warning application. In some communities, there are large sirens that begin to sound when a tornado is spotted. Still, because of the unpredictable nature of tornadoes, the death count from these storms is remains high.

Storm chasers are people who actually seek out tornadoes—some for the thrill, but many are scientists gathering information. It is a very dangerous activity, for the ability of a tornado to suddenly shift paths or split into "sisters" can never be discounted. In May 2012, an experienced scientist by the name of Tim Samaras was killed, along with his crew, as he followed a storm in Oklahoma. Despite many years' experience in the field, Samaras could not evade the fast-moving tornado when the funnel shifted and headed straight for the car.

INTRODUCTION

Part I of this book looks into the land and people who lived in the communities of Sandusky and Lorain. The geology, history and economic structures of Sandusky and Lorain are generally explained.

Part II recounts what happened over a period of four days: July 28, 1924, and the following three days of shock, despair and heroic rescues. When the F4-strength black funnel swooped out from the sky and careened, helter skelter, across the land and lake, the citizens of Lorain and Sandusky reacted as all humans would when their world literally crumbles around them.

Caught completely off guard, they fell into the embrace of a killer storm born from monster weather systems colliding over Lake Erie. The tornado funnel hit the two shore communities—Sandusky first and then, twenty-six minutes later, Lorain—before hopscotching across pastures and farms bordering the lakeshore of northern Ohio. It capriciously touched down three more times to destroy property and buildings in rural communities east of Cleveland and killed three farmers before the funnel rose back into the storm clouds and disappeared to the east, leaving behind death and destruction.

The Conclusion addresses these two communities today. Sandusky and Lorain each survived the devastation of the tornado, cleaned up the remains of their proud cities and, in some cases, literally rebuilt parts of their communities on the debris left by the storm.

When you visit these cities, you are very aware of Lake Erie. Its waves lap the shoreline; the cooling breeze you feel comes off the water. Lake Erie is enormous, mysterious and a very real player in the lives of the people who live on its shores. June 28, 1924, was just one day in the thousands of years the lake has existed.

Just one day—but a very important one if you were among the dead, injured or mourners of lost loved ones. If you know about the day the monstrous tornado raced off the water and onto land, you might scan the horizon where sky meets water and see the world with different eyes.

Part I

YESTERDAY AND TODAY

Lake Erie and its sibling lakes of Superior, Michigan, Huron and Ontario are children of the last ice age, a reoccurring geological event in the earth's history. The last ice age began about 100,000 years ago, and with its end, about 10,000 to 14,000 years ago, the glacial ice sheets, sometimes two to three miles thick, began to withdraw and crawl north. The great stress of such massive ice sheets worked as a sculptor on the soil and bedrock of the earth below, slowly carving out the topography of land as we see it today.

Over the millennia, the Laurentide ice sheet would move south from the North Pole and cover a great deal of what is now North America. Each time this occurred, the force and weight of the glaciers would scoop out softer areas of earth and create basins. Five of those mammoth basins would eventually develop into what we call the Great Lakes. As the glaciers receded north, their melting water filled the basins with aptly named "melt" water.

To understand this process more clearly, envision the glaciers as scoops, moving over the terrain of the Northern Hemisphere. The pressure of the glaciers was not constant, and the underlying rock surface changed from place to place. As a result, the earth was scooped up, creating the lakes with all their different depths and shapes. Consequently, the western portion of Lake Erie is much shallower than the eastern end, but the western side enjoys the addition of many more islands.

The border between the United States and Canada is off shore about thirty miles in Lake Erie. One can boat back and forth without going through customs. Lake Erie borders four states—New York, Pennsylvania,

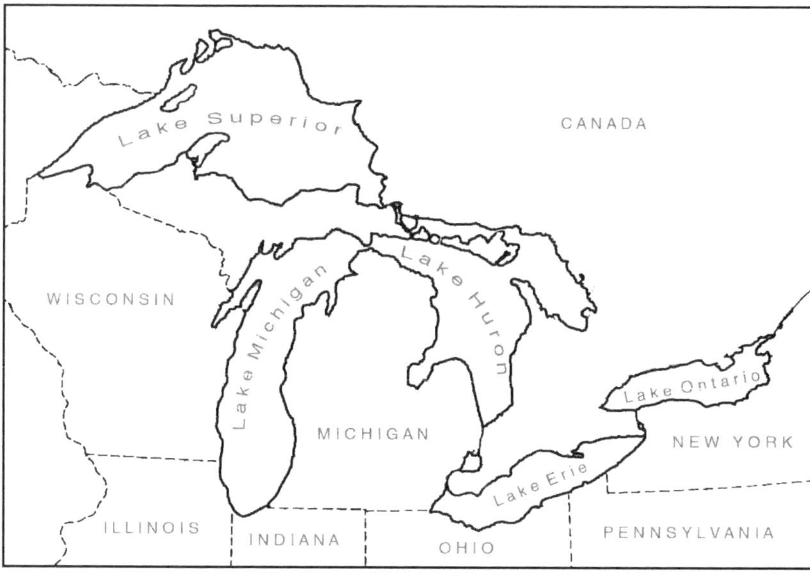

Great Lakes map. *Courtesy of the author.*

Ohio and Michigan—and is fed by the Detroit River, itself an overspill of the higher Great Lakes of Michigan, Huron and Superior. Many smaller rivers also contribute to the water intake, such as the Cuyahoga in Cleveland and the Black River in Lorain. On its eastern edge, Lake Erie spills into Lake Ontario, which, in turn, feeds the Niagara River and then Niagara Falls.

Lake Erie lies at 42.2 degrees north and 81.2 degrees west and is 571 feet above sea level. At 9,910 square miles, it is the fourth-largest Great Lake in surface but the shallowest in depth. It is also the eleventh-largest lake in the world—or twelfth, depending on how one measures surface area.

The borders of the lake we recognize as Erie are only about four thousand years old. Because of prior glacial events, the original lake was much larger than the one we see today. The ancient shores extended outward about eight to ten miles from our modern shoreline. The original shorelines, now inland, have cut into the land, making perfect spots for Indian trails, followed by wagon paths and then roads for automobiles. Route 20 heading west from Cleveland follows the shoreline of the ancient lake.

Lake Erie is famous for weather-related phenomena. This is mainly due to three different, but related, conditions. First, the lake is shallow, and a shallow lake is more likely to experience high waves and warmer water. Second, Lake Erie's placement on the continent of North America is also significant in meteorological terms. Warm winds from the Gulf of Mexico travel upward and to the east, passing over the lake one thousand miles to the north. These warm-weather systems often collide with cold-weather systems heading southeast from Canada. Cold fronts from Canada are more likely to interact with warm fronts coming north from the Gulf of Mexico. Third, the warm water reacts with the air temperature of incoming fronts in a way that makes the atmosphere far more prone to violent storms in both summer and winter.

These weather events occur most often in November, when the lake water is still quite warm, making it particularly hazardous to be on the water. One result of this trio of conditions is lake-effect snow. When winds from the west cross over the lake and the temperature of the water and the temperature of the air hit a certain range, the result is snowstorm. Anyone from Toledo, Ohio, to Buffalo, New York, can describe a Lake Erie snowstorm, famous for profuse amounts of wet snow. If high winds are added to the mix, the lake can be buffeted by gale-force winds that are lethal in intensity. November is the high point for terrible storms on all of the Great Lakes, and Lake Erie is no exception. "November Witch" is an old term for the storms of November.

In the summer, the mix of location, water and air temperatures and water depth can result in similar violent storms. However, because of the heat, the storms are more localized and might become cyclonic, with super cells creating funnels, waterspouts or both. These storms are only a little less deadly than the November gales.

Another phenomenon that is peculiar to Cleveland is a mirage that occasionally hovers over the lake. It is an atmospheric, light-related event. It appears as if Detroit, Michigan, far to the north, is suspended over the water. Many people have reported witnessing this mirage. The optical illusion has detractors and supporters, but some meteorologists say it can actually occur if all conditions are correct.

Not in dispute are the unexplained giant waves that have hit Cleveland and the northern Ohio shore three times in the last 150 years. The first one was on June 23, 1882. Just after dawn, many people reported seeing dark gray streaks in the sky over Lake Erie and hearing a large boom, which they attributed to thunder. The lake remained smooth and glassy until, suddenly, the water reared back like a small tsunami before rushing toward land.

At exactly 6:20 a.m., a nine-foot wall of water smashed into the Cleveland shoreline and pushed logs and heavy debris inland. The force of the wave tossed barges onto dry docks and caused damage to the industrial plants along the waterfront. Small boats were upended or crushed against docks.

On June 1, 1942, the same scenario was repeated. A similar, unexpected wave hit Cleveland and the north shore, bringing in a huge mass of dead fish. On a calm, windless day, the large wave hit without warning, and this time there was loss of life. Eight people perished as a result of the peculiar wave, and once again, the origin of the wave was unknown. It was determined that there was no earthquake, thunderstorm or violent winds over the lake. People said the lake had been unusually calm that day.

On July 1, 2012, a rogue wave hit the beach in Lake County, not far from Cleveland. Three teenagers on shore saw it coming but didn't have time to run. Within seconds, they were swept into the water with such speed and force that in a minute they were a half mile from shore. Luckily, a man on a jet ski saw what happened and managed to rescue them. Once again, it was a beautiful day, and there was no warning of what was coming.

There have been many theories about the formation of these rogue waves. The most popular one is that a thunderstorm out on the lake caused the wave, but modern theories have included a meteorite hitting the water or an underground explosion of gas.

In the nineteenth century, Lake Erie became very busy with boat traffic that shipped goods east to west and vice versa; additionally, the lake was beautiful and popular for all types of recreation. Despite all its good points, Lake Erie was getting a reputation for being treacherous.

The reputation was well deserved. The Great Lakes Shipwreck Museum in Paradise, Michigan, has calculated that approximately six thousand ships have sunk in the Great Lakes, with a calculated loss of thirty thousand lives. It is estimated that two thousand shipwrecks lie on the bottom of Lake Erie, many perfectly preserved by the cold, fresh water.

Why so many wrecks? There are many reasons.

By the nineteenth century, the lake was already a major shipping route, and with a great quantity of boats on the water, the number of collisions grew. Without modern navigation tools, boats often collided in heavy fog or bad weather, and once in distress, there wasn't much of a way to communicate the problem.

Safety on the water didn't meet the standards we expect today. Wooden masts snapped in heavy winds, making it impossible to move in heavy storms. Steam engines exploded, igniting fires, especially dangerous and deadly on wooden vessels far out on the lake. Signal lights were lanterns, not electrical beacons, and could easily be doused by high waves or pelting rain.

But the greatest reason boats sank so often in Lake Erie was due to Lake Erie storms. The lake is famous for gales and high waves. Also, the prevailing winds over the lake come from the west and are often quite strong. The lake tends to be shallow in many spots. During a bad storm, these winds can alter the lakebeds and change the locations of sandbars. If a ship survived the storm, there was always the danger of foundering on a newly created sandbar.

One such wreck was the *Sarah Sheldon*. This steam-driven boat was a "local gal." It was built of wood in what is now Lorain by the E.M. Peck Company, and its engines and boilers were constructed in Cleveland. Its main purpose was to carry industrial goods from one Great Lakes port to another. The *Sarah Sheldon*'s maiden voyage was in 1872.

Its luck ran out thirty-three years later. During a violent gale, it struck a reef and broke up only six hundred feet from shore. Two members of the crew died. The skeletal wreck is now in twenty feet of water and is a popular dive site in Lake Erie.

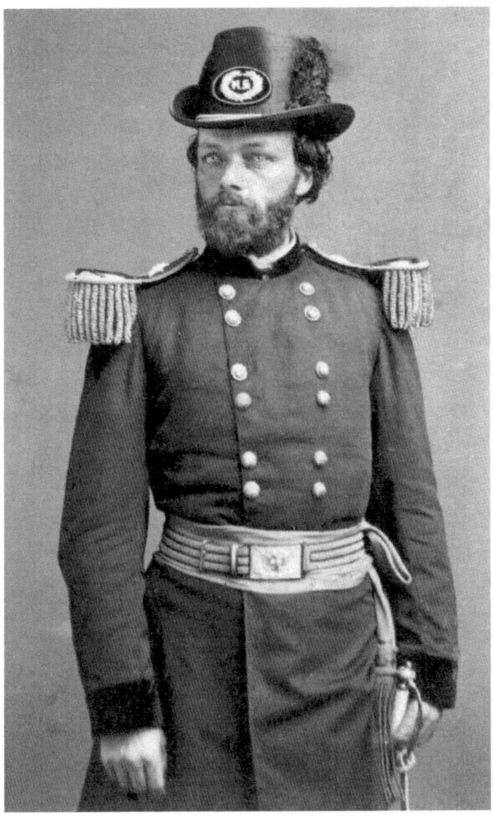

General Quincy Adams Gillmore, a Civil War general whose family farm became part of Lakeview Park. *Ohio Historical Society.*

Other shipwrecks have become quite famous. At least eight wrecks are off the shores of Lorain, and another eight to ten are north of Sandusky and in the waters around the western islands.

One of the most famous wrecks occurred in the late hours of the night in 1868. During a rainy night with poor visibility, the passenger ship *Morning Star* collided with the bark *Cortland*, heavy with iron ore. Both ships had night lanterns, but the rain might have doused the flames. Both ships sank within the hour. Although there were survivors, approximately forty people died. The wreck lies eight miles north of Lorain in about sixty-five feet of water.

A coal schooner named after distinguished Civil War general Quincy A. Gillmore sank near Kelly's Island, near

Sandusky, in 1870 in a violent storm, and the wreck is still in very good condition today. After the tornado of 1924 hit Sandusky, it returned to its original path across the lake and came very close to Kelly's Island, moving near the ship lying on the bottom of the lake. The tornado then traveled twenty-six miles to Lorain and made landfall at Lakeview Park with deadly intensity. Coincidentally, Lakeview Park was once part of the farm owned by the family of General Quincy A. Gillmore.

Another famous storm was the Black Friday Storm of October 20, 1916. Three converging high-pressure systems created a monster storm that developed hurricane-strength winds. In Lake Erie, many ships battled the storm, but four lost the fight. The *D.L. Filer*, the *James B. Colgate*, the *Marshall Butters* and the *Merida* all sank, taking at least fifty-eight sailors to their deaths.

The perfect storm of the Great Lakes occurred in November 1913. Cold air from Canada rushed southeast, while warm, moist air from the Gulf of Mexico rapidly blew northeast. The two weather fronts collided in the month of November over the Great Lakes and then stalled, creating a violent storm. This storm truly lived up to the sobriquet "November Witch." Many people referred to it as the White Hurricane because it was a combination blizzard and hurricane.

A typical storm of this type lasts about four to five hours, but this monster blasted the Great Lakes and the ships caught on the water for over twenty-two hours. Lake Huron took the brunt of the storm, but Lake Erie had its share of disasters. The snow, gale-force winds and giant waves sent 250 sailors to icy, watery graves. Twenty-five ships sank before the storm moved into Canada.

Lorain did not escape the fury of the November storm. Fourteen-foot waves pounded the shoreline of the city, causing flooding in some parts of town. Six- to eight-foot drifts of snow blocked the roads, impeding almost all forms of travel. Before the storm ended, more than three hundred people had died in Ohio's north shore communities.

It is interesting to note that people in 1913 complained that there had been no warning about the monster storm heading their way, and for those sailors who did suspect, many ignored the red flags on the Great Lakes. In 1924, a similar convergence of competing weather fronts merged over Lake Erie, but it was June, and the result was the tornado that destroyed much of Sandusky and Lorain. And, as in 1913, there were many complaints about not having any advance warning.

The history of the lands surrounding Lake Erie is as violent as the geology and weather. Before European exploration of the Great Lakes region, there were numerous Native American tribes that made their homes along the shores of Lake Erie. The predominant tribal groups were called the Eries. These Native American groups were relatively peaceful, but more aggressive Indians moving west toward their land attacked them. The Eries, along with other tribes, eventually submitted to the warlike Iroquois Confederation native to the East Coast and came under Iroquois rule.

By the 1600s, French explorers were making their way into the region. French fur trappers working the forests around the lake in the eighteenth century were astounded at the wildlife. In their diaries, they recounted tales of being stalked by panthers who slinked through the thick forests to hunt. The trappers watched the big cats move down to the shore to drink the pure, crystalline water. Impressed by the panthers, the French named the body of water *Lac du Chat*, or "Lake of the Cat."

The Erie Indians were the first to tell the white trappers about the monster that lived in the lake. French trappers first sighted the Lake Erie monster, later officially named Bessie, in 1793 and added their stories to the Indian legends. Over the next two hundred years, the sightings continued. All the accounts describe a remarkably similar creature—something thirty to sixty feet long resembling a snake, with a small head and arm-like appendages or fins.

English settlers moving west slowly displaced the French fur trappers as the most numerous pioneers in the area, and they reported several sightings of Bessie. They referred to the vast lake as the home of the Eries in honor of the American tribe living on the lakeshore. With the Anglicization of the area, Lac du Chat became Lake Erie.

As more and more settlers moved west into the Ohio territory, the area became of interest politically, economically and militarily. Bordering both Canada and the United States, the ownership of Lake Erie became a bone of contention between Great Britain and the United States.

The situation came to a head during the War of 1812. On the morning of September 10, 1813, Admiral Oliver Hazard Perry and his fleet made up of 557 sailors on nine vessels met the British near Put-In-Bay, an island on Lake Erie. The battle was fierce, and the booming guns could be heard at the mouth of the Black River, where settlers anxiously awaited news.

Perry commanded the flagship of the fleet and hoisted a flag with the slogan "Don't Give up the Ship." But when his ship was irreparably

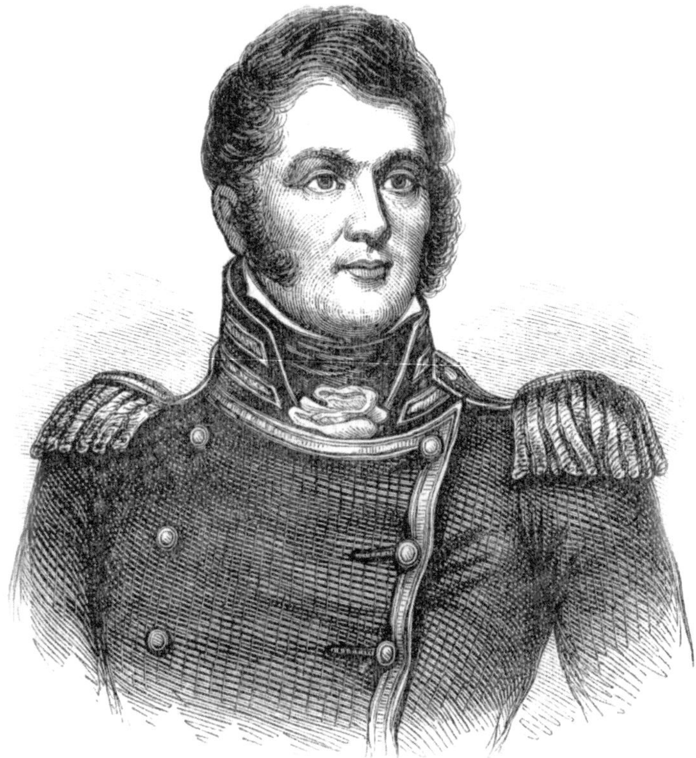

Commodore Oliver Hazard Perry, the hero of the Battle of Lake Erie, War of 1812. *Ohio Historical Society.*

damaged, Perry gave in to practicality and switched from the *Laurence* to the USS *Niagara* and went on to win the battle. He sent out a scribbled message to the high command that read:

> *Dear General,*
> *We have met the enemy and they are ours. Two ships, two brigs, one schooner, and one sloop. Yours with great respect and esteem.*
> *O.H. Perry*

It was a bloody battle for both sides, but the twenty-nine Americans who died, and the ninety-four wounded, suffered for a good cause. Their sacrifice prevented the British from moving into the Ohio River Valley and aided greatly in the United States' victory over Great Britain in the War of 1812.

Between the War of 1812 and 1860, the north shore of Ohio saw another immigrant group start to arrive in significant numbers. German immigrants, desiring either more religious freedom or political participation, began to settle the north shore. This large influx of Germans is still reflected in the population in the area today. Although Smith is a common English last name, many people with the last name of Smith were originally Schmidts from Germany who Anglicized their last name as they became more absorbed in the culture of the United States. The street names around Lorain, such as Berlin Road, also reflect this German heritage.

Twenty years later, the borders between the United States and Canada were set, but a new issue—that of slavery—had become a heated topic. In 1833, Canada outlawed slavery, and as a result, many American slaves tried to make the hazardous trip to freedom using what we now call the Underground Railroad. Sandusky, a prominent fishing and shipping village west of Lorain and Cleveland, was one of the last jumping-off points to Canada and freedom. There are still "safe houses" one can see where runaway slaves were sheltered until the Civil War. Harriet Beecher Stowe, in her famous book *Uncle Tom's Cabin*, used Sandusky as the last stop on the way to Canada and freedom for her characters. Lorain, then known as the village of Charleston, was STOP 100 on the Underground Railroad.

With its traditional long opposition to slavery, it is not surprising that Ohio stood with the Union during the Civil War. Ohio sent 300,000 men to fight, and 7,000 died in the war. A prisoner of war camp was built in Sandusky Bay to house Confederate soldiers.

Quincy Adams Gillmore, whose family owned a farm in Lorain that would later be sold into the Lakeview Park complex, graduated first in his class at West Point. He played a key role in the Civil War when troops under his command were instrumental in leading the siege and eventual capture of Fort Pulaski in Georgia. He became a general and later had a ship named after him.

It should be noted that the three greatest Union generals of the Civil War—Ulysses S. Grant, William T. Sherman and Philip H. Sheridan—all hailed from Ohio. Grant would go on to become president of the United States. In all subsequent wars and police actions throughout the world, Ohio men and women have participated with valor and courage.

The growing industries of northern Ohio supported the Civil War effort and, following the war, the emergent industrial nation. Lake Erie, and the Black River that flowed into it, enabled the creation of the city of Lorain as a major industrial and port center. Thousands of immigrants from all over the world poured into the city to work in the mills, shipyards and factories. This great influx of workers in the nineteenth century continued into the twentieth century.

Sandusky, twenty-six miles to the west, was the embarkation point for all the islands of western Lake Erie, islands people were starting to visit every summer. It was also an important railroad center.

So what does this have to do with the tornado of 1924?

Well, it sets the stage for the catastrophe that occurred.

The year 1924 wasn't so long ago.

If you are in your nineties, you may have been alive at that time. Many people today had parents or grandparents who vividly recalled that fateful year. If we had a time machine and could travel back to 1924, we would discover a world both familiar and yet very different from how we live, think, perceive and respond to events that shape our lives.

So much of 1924 is still here if you know where to look.

As one travels to Cedar Point in Sandusky, a famous tourist destination for amusement park aficionados, visitors first notice the large expanse of sky and clouds, a montage of blue and white not found in many other places. The closer you drive toward Lake Erie, the highway morphs into a long thoroughfare catering to the three million tourists who visit the Point each year. Motels, restaurants, gas stations and amusement parks line both sides of the road. However, if one watches carefully, crowded between fast-food restaurants, billboards and fences, he or she might spot a tall, circular structure resembling the tower of a castle. The structure almost seems to be hiding, as if embarrassed to have survived into this modern, raucous world.

Is it part of a medieval theme park catering to tourists?

No. This relic of a bygone age is a silo, once an important structure on a farm. It held the farmer's corn and grain. The silo's forgotten presence is a reminder that this land was all farm country ninety years ago—the best farm country in the world. The silo is very old and probably was standing, filled with grain, on June 28, 1924.

Behind it, through rough and rural overgrowth, run railroad tracks. For the last 160 years, these tracks have anchored the United States from east to west and back again. The railroads were the great land-based shipping arteries of the United States in the nineteenth and early twentieth centuries. Even today, as you drive down a narrow, rutted farm lane seemingly going nowhere, you may suddenly find yourself in a long line of cars stopped by crossing signals ahead. Peer out the window and you will see an impossibly long train amble along the tracks heading west to Chicago or east to Buffalo.

Suddenly, ninety years slip away, and it is 1924 once again.

To better understand the cataclysm of June 28, 1924, we have to take a good look at the world at the beginning of the last century. The first quarter of the twentieth century was witness to two devastating international events. World War I began in 1914, and the United States entered in April 1917. It was called the Great War because no one could envision another war on such a scale. When it ended in November 1918, millions worldwide were dead, borders of nations were often changed and the monarchies of Russia, Germany and Austria had collapsed.

Lorain, with its large German population, was especially sensitive to the implications of war with Germany. Many immigrants worked at American Shipbuilding, which had just received a $56 million order for sixty-six vessels to man the United States Emergency Fleet. Anti-German feeling wasn't rabid, but one saloon owner recklessly went too far when he kept a large photograph of Kaiser Wilhelm over his bar. A group of outraged citizens, probably of German descent, entered his bar and tore down the offensive photo of the German emperor. Mission accomplished, it is quite possible that they stayed on for a drink.

Immediately after the end of the Great War, the Spanish flu epidemic struck. It was a deadly form of the flu virus, and it killed more people worldwide than all the numbers who died in the four years of the Great War. Northern Ohio was not immune to this scourge. In 1918, at least two hundred people died in Lorain alone.

For some reason, the virus was most virulent among the young and healthy, and it killed quickly.

"Well at breakfast, sick at lunch, dead by dinner" was a popular phrase that described the illness.

Finally, by 1924, the war was six years in the past, and the Spanish flu had disappeared after killing millions. These twin demons of annihilation were defeated, and people were optimistic about the future and determined not to look back. It was the Roaring Twenties, and the United States was on the road to prosperity.

In northern Ohio, prosperity meant steel mills, shipbuilding and railroads, working to capacity and flourishing in trade on the Great Lakes. Lorain grew and prospered with the boom in these industries. Large immigrant populations uprooted by the war, eager to find work, arrived by the thousands and settled in Lorain. People worked hard, and they played hard.

These people knew how difficult survival could be. Still, they were optimistic and eager for all the pleasures of modern life. They were grateful to be in the United States and proud to support their families and put food on the table. This pride of self carried over easily into pride in their communities, churches and neighborhoods.

To the west of Lorain, in Sandusky, this prosperity took a more recreational form. Large ferries took people to the western islands for vacations and holiday retreats. Cedar Point and the nearby islands were becoming vacation destinations for many people, who were now getting that newfangled time off called vacation.

So how are we similar to them?

Well, for one thing, all adults, with the exception of convicted felons and the insane, were allowed to vote. Four years earlier, Congress had passed the Nineteenth Amendment enfranchising women. Unfortunately, both men and women were not permitted to drink alcohol. Prohibition, making liquor illegal, was in full force, also having passed into law in 1920.

Electricity was a part of their lives. This miraculous innovation had been around for fifty years. In 1924, electrical grids were almost universal in the cities. Because towns like Lorain and Sandusky were on the populated northern shore of Ohio, most streets had electric-powered streetlights. If you lived in one of the sleepy farming communities to the south, you were still probably waiting to be hooked up to the electric grid. Nightfall in rural areas usually brought a darkness dispersed only by kerosene lamps or gaslight.

Along with electric lights, electricity brought modern entertainment. If you had electricity, you probably had a radio. Used not only for music, radio programs were also a main source of information and news. Only newspapers, usually delivered both in the morning and the evening, beat out the radio in informing people about what was happening in their communities.

One of the most exciting forms of entertainment was listening to music on a victrola, the earliest form of record player. By 1924, the Wickens Funeral Home had moved out of the Wickens Building and to a new location. The

Wickens Building now was home to the Wickens Furniture Store. In 1924, victrolas could be purchased at the Wickens Furiniture Store, located next door to the four-story State Theater Building, previously known as the Wagner Opera House.

George Wickens, who had started his career as both an undertaker and a businessman, knew how to push a product. The victrolas cost twenty-five dollars each, a princely sum for most people. For those who could not pay that amount of money all at once, Mr. Wickens would accept one dollar down and fifty cents a week as a guaranteed sale.

Another wonderful invention was the telephone. Invented by Alexander Graham Bell, it had been around for about thirty years and was becoming a popular necessity. But phones in 1924 looked nothing like our phones today. There was an earpiece you held to your ear and a mouthpiece on the main box, which was usually nailed to the wall. Five to seven families would share one line, aptly named a "party line."

If you wanted to make a phone call, you would dial the operator, and she would put through your call. To receive an incoming call, you would hear rings, and it was necessary to count to see if it was for you. Each family on the party line would have a specific number of rings. A person would pick up the phone when he heard his assigned number of rings, but any of one's fellow party line connections could pick up and listen. Eavesdropping was frowned on but almost impossible to stop. Needless to say, juicy gossip didn't stay secret for long.

A few lucky families had automobiles, and going "for a drive" was a popular form of entertainment. More and more roads were being paved to accommodate Henry Ford's Model T, affectionately called the "Tin Lizzie," but a country dirt road was usually a pothole nightmare.

Only twenty years before, in 1904, the City of Lorain had passed an ordinance prohibiting cars and bicycles from traveling faster than eight miles an hour. There was a great fear of collision with horse-drawn vehicles of all types, especially fire wagons. A building had recently burned to the ground when the fire wagon, trying to avoid other traffic, got stuck in the mud and the horses were unable to pull it free. In 1912, the city decided to pave over the bricks on Broadway with asphalt in concession to more and more automobiles and the trolley lines.

By 1924, a main highway went through town, and honking a hand horn was a good way to let pedestrians know you were coming. Horses were still in use to pull wagons, but they were slowly disappearing in that capacity. It must be assumed that automobile drivers and horses had learned to accommodate one another. Drivers used hand signals to indicate a turn. Going for a recreational ride was becoming popular among the prosperous. Thirty miles an hour was considered a reckless but very good clip.

As nice as cars were, they weren't used for long-distance travel. There was no interstate highway system, and in some places, the roads were simply impassible. Traveling from town to town was usually done by trolley. If you wanted to travel farther afield, say from Cleveland to Pittsburg, you would take the train. Motorbuses were in their infancy. The Yellow Bus Manufacturing Company was founded in 1923.

Planes were novelties used for entertainment at county fairs. Stunt pilots put on shows, flying across the fields, sometimes with daredevils walking on the wings. Accidents were frequent. The United States government had just started using planes for airmail. To send a letter by airmail, a writer had to purchase a special stamp that was more expensive than the average stamp.

For the intrepid traveler who wanted to leave the country, he traveled by boat. A transatlantic crossing by ocean liner from New York to London took just under a week. A trip to the Mediterranean could take up to two weeks.

Refrigerators were actually iceboxes—metal boxes with legs that kept food cold with huge blocks of ice. The ice was delivered every few days by the iceman and frequently came by horse-drawn cart. By 1924, most city dwellers had electrically cooled iceboxes, but they were small compared to what we have today.

There were no supermarkets. Most housewives walked down to the grocery store daily to restock their iceboxes and cupboards. Small A&P grocery stores, the forerunners of supermarkets, might be found in larger towns. Grocers delivered if you were unable to pick up your food.

Dairy products, which the milkmen delivered, such as milk, butter and eggs, arrived every morning before dawn and were left by the front door. In many areas, his truck was a wagon pulled by a horse. Milk was delivered each morning in glass bottles, which a family would put back after use. Often, produce was sold door-to-door direct from the farm.

A housewife had to know how to kill, gut and pluck a chicken if she decided not to use the services of her butcher. It is interesting to note that in 1924, many city people still had chicken coops and small farm animals in their backyards. Zoning laws didn't begin to change until the middle of the last century.

The concept of fast food, or convenience foods, didn't exist. The microwave was sixty years in the future for common use. If a housewife wanted ground beef, her butcher would grind it for her while she waited, or she would take a steak home and grind it herself. Stores tended to sell one type of product—i.e., the butcher for meat, the fish market for fish, the bakery for bread. Produce markets specialized in fruits and vegetables. General grocery stores carried the rest of the goods on a grocery list.

If you wanted a special cake the bakery could not provide, you would bake it from scratch. Mixes were not invented for another thirty years and would not be in common use until the 1960s. Canned food was sold in stores, but frozen food was almost unheard of. Your choices were fresh or canned.

Most women canned food themselves, although in the home this was a misnomer; rather than tin cans, bottles were used. In the fall, housewives would "put up" their vegetables, fruits and jams for winter use. This involved boiling bottles to sterilize, making the product to be canned and then sealing bottles with wax. Everyone feared making a mistake. If the bottles weren't airtight, there was the danger of botulism poisoning.

Housewives didn't have automatic dishwashers, or clothes-washing machines or dryers. Washday was a long, tedious effort in the basement followed by hauling the wet laundry outside to be hung on the line. Then, of course, everything had to be ironed because there wasn't such a thing as wrinkle-free clothing or linen.

On the bright side, a person today would be pleasantly surprised by the prices. In 1924, sliced ham was selling for $0.29 a pound. Stamps were $0.02 apiece. A cup of coffee cost $0.05. A man's suit could be found for $24.99. A nice dress cost $8.00. Synthetic fibers as we know them did not exist for the most part. Textiles were pretty much limited to silk, wool, cotton and linen. Men and women both wore hats when they went out. Cotton and wool were the most common fabrics for clothes. Women wore silk stockings held up with garters, as were men's socks.

Bathing suits for men and woman were made of wool, and for the men, you could get a two-piece bathing suit for seven dollars. The one-piece suit had a T-shirt attached—wool, of course. Most women would also wear black wool knee socks with their bathing suits, along with fetching little white caps that kept their hair in place. For those who really went out for a long swim, bathing caps that kept the ears dry were worn. Modesty was always a concern.

Sneakers did not exist. All shoes were made of leather and were manufactured in the United States. In fact, all clothes, except designer outfits from Paris, were made in the United States. The idea that most clothing would someday be made in Asia would be unbelievable to people in 1924.

When considering the low prices, keep in mind that the pay scale was much lower. According to the IRS, the average net income in Ohio per capita was $3,357.85. That works out to $64.00 a week per person. This was considered a very good wage, and people flocked to northern Ohio to take advantage of this new prosperity.

Like today's teenagers, young people back in 1924 walked downtown to the movies to see the latest shows. In 1924, Lorain boasted seven theaters. Movies still lacked sound, but the orchestra pit of each theater had musicians who often entertained between the short feature films and provided sound effects for the movie. There was no air conditioning, but sitting in the dark could be a cool respite on a hot summer day.

Silent movies were the rage, and people filled theaters, eager for entertainment. The old vaudeville theaters were slowly transforming into real modern theaters, but as late as 1914—just ten years before the tornado leveled the State Street Theater and killed more people in one theater in Ohio history than ever before—one of the more popular events was Farmyard Night, where livestock were given away as door prizes. Many a lucky patron went home with a new chicken for the coop or leashed a lamb or goat down the main street to the trolley and home.

But in recounting the "modern" conveniences the citizens of 1924 enjoyed, we must also examine what they lacked. Life expectancy for a woman was sixty-one and half, three years more than for a man. Half of all women still gave birth at home rather than in hospitals.

Diphtheria and typhoid fever were real concerns. Only twenty-three years earlier, the city of Lorain had celebrated its first year without any deaths from typhoid fever. It was considered a victory for the newly updated water supply system, but no one took the better water for granted. Many grandparents still remembered when at least ten deaths a year from typhoid fever were common.

Because Alexander Fleming would not discover penicillin until 1928, death from infection was a very real threat. Death in childbirth was a frightening possibility for both mothers and children. Blood poisoning from infections and childhood diseases like measles, mumps and whooping cough were often lethal.

On a high point, Kimberley Clark Corporation came out with Kleenex in 1924. Three years prior, Johnson and Johnson had brought out the first band-aid. Some cough syrups still contained cocaine and were sold over the counter. Cocaine was also found in Coca-Cola, an exciting new drink.

Unlike our age, troubled with fears of cancer and heart disease, the citizens of 1924 were far more anxious about catching tuberculosis, which was a common cause of death. Or worse, in the hot months of summer, people agonized over catching polio. Franklin Delano Roosevelt, who would later become president of the United States, caught polio in 1924. The disease left him crippled and wheelchair bound for the rest of his life.

YESTERDAY AND TODAY

By modern standards, it was a time of isolation and insulation, but people in 1924 would be shocked by our assessment; after all, they listened to radios, enjoyed silent movies, talked to family and friends on their party line telephones and traveled, if fortunate, in their new automobiles.

Space travel, radar, televisions, computers, I-pods, cellphones and video games were not even imagined, except by a few in the budding industry called science fiction. Comic books were very popular among science fiction fans, but the exciting "tools" used in the comic books were considered fantasy to their readers.

Our world is one where people watch tsunamis half a world away in real time and news is presented twenty-four/seven. We accept this type of coverage, and the subsequent anxiety that arises is the price we have to pay for safety. It is hard to imagine a time when everyone wasn't on high alert, especially about weather dangers lurking in the coming hours.

In 1924, weather reporting, if not in its infancy, was certainly an inexact science. The saying was: "If you want to know the weather, stick your head out the window and take a look." On June 27, 1924, no one except a few budding meteorologists knew there would be two weather systems, one high pressure and one low pressure, possibly colliding over Lake Erie in the next twenty-four hours. Violent storms were a fact of life. People knew about, and had experienced, tornadoes, but these swirling black funnels were not understood and impossible to predict, so why worry about them?

You knew a storm was coming when you saw it approaching. The potential severity of the storm was a good guess. Farmers took a look at their cows to see if they were jumpy; city dwellers opted for experience. Since television had not been invented, there was no Weather Channel to check.

Today, if a bad storm is threatening, television stations go to full coverage with Doppler radar. Meteorologists pinpoint funnels in real time and tell you when these weather threats will arrive on your doorstep, almost street by street. The modern world, sometimes so intrusive and bewildering with its massive info glut, protects us to a large degree with knowledge of danger. In cases like hurricanes and blizzards, it isn't ignorance that leads to fatalities but ignoring the warnings to seek protection.

In 1924, people were sheltered from the knowledge of approaching danger, much to their ultimate grief and loss. Their very ignorance of what was happening in another state, another town or even down the road a mile or two prevented them from taking steps to run for safety.

This lack of knowledge wasn't a choice they made. In their world, the inventions we take for granted simply hadn't been discovered. Even the concepts of those inventions hadn't been discussed, unless, perhaps, by scientists.

So if 1924 was a different world from ours, we must remember that each new generation works on what the past generation has given them. Sometimes it takes a disaster to see the importance of expanding knowledge and awareness.

June 28, 1924, was the type of summer day people anticipated with pleasure during the long, damp Ohio winter. A high-pressure system over Lake Erie was creating strong breezes, cooling the inhabitants of the lakeshore towns, and since it was a Saturday, many people were off from work. Winter was gone; now it was summer, and those who were able packed picnics and went to the many beaches along the lake. It was a day for swimming, fishing and sailing.

The heat and humidity rose with every passing hour, but people who had jobs or errands were downtown shopping. Unlike today, stores closed on Sundays, so it was important to get what you needed by closing time on Saturday.

Blue laws—legislation prohibiting shops, theaters and other forms of entertainment venues from opening on Sunday—were strongly enforced. Of course, the sale of liquor was illegal. The year 1924 was a time when the values of church, family and country were strictly respected. People were expected to go to church on Sunday and then spend time with family and friends.

In 1926, several theater owners in Lorain challenged the blue laws and were immediately threatened with arrest. However, as people expanded their views of what a "day of rest" encompassed, the theaters eventually began to open on Sundays. Out on the countless farms that defined rural Ohio, the work didn't cease because it was the weekend. Fields needed to be tended, livestock fed and watered and cows milked. Farmers went about their business as they had for one hundred years.

On the morning of June 28, 1924, there was little sign of rain, but everyone commented on how still and sultry it was. Even the birds seemed quieter. However, it was summer, so this kind of weather was to be expected. Both on the farms and in the cities and small towns, people were preparing for the Fourth of July, just six days away. Just like today, there was a lot to do.

If they could speak to us, they would say that theirs was a busy, modern, bustling world. And they would be right. The people of Lorain and Sandusky on June 28, 1924, were enjoying the fruits of modern innovation. But what they had available was not enough to save them.

The clouds expanding over eastern Iowa were racing east. It was a low-pressure weather system, and by the end of the day, it would collide head-on with the high-pressure system over Lake Erie.

That collision would forge a killer tornado.

Part II
THE TORNADO

Day One: June 28, 1924

12:40 a.m., Northeastern Iowa

The night was typical for Iowa in late June—warm and sultry. Thousands of feet above the black, loamy farm fields, a barometric depression system, born in the hot and humid Gulf of Mexico, was finally lumbering east. It brought light rain, which began to fall over the rich, sun-warmed earth, and the corn—now rising up to farmers' knees, considered optimal height six days before the Fourth of July—was actually bending to the east as the wind grew stronger. Anyone still awake and up to venturing a guess would predict a good storm over Lake Erie, hundreds of miles due east, by late afternoon.

6:00 a.m., South Shore of Lake Erie in Ohio

With a high-pressure system settled over northern Ohio, Saturday, June 28, 1924, started out with great promise for a sizzling summer weekend. Farmers, along with other early risers, were struck by the stifling heat and unnatural stillness. The weather report projected a few early showers followed by a lovely summer day, and exactly as predicted, several rainy patches moved in from the west, showered the earth, added more moisture to the overwhelming humidity and then disappeared. The sky cleared to a robin's egg blue as the morning progressed.

Many people felt an air of expectancy, but no one could put a finger on the cause. Perhaps it was anticipation for the coming Fourth of July, with all the attendant parades, picnics and fireworks.

There was additional excitement in Lorain, Ohio. A train accident in the industrial section of the city had everyone's attention. Someone had erred during the night and left the Nickel Plate swing bridge upright. By the time the engineer of an oncoming locomotive saw the problem, it was too late to stop the train, and the first cars plunged into the Black River beneath the bridge.

No one was killed, but the sight of the train cars stuck in the Black River was the talk of the town. Anyone who was able went out to the bridge to see the accident. It was a special draw for young boys who owned bicycles; half the male teenagers in the city had pedaled out to see the accident.

The Nickel Plate Bridge was near the original settlement of Lorain. After the American Revolution, a small community of pioneers moved into the area at the junction of the Black River and Lake Erie. These men and women were looking for land to settle, and at thirty cents an acre, the northern Ohio territory was a good deal. It was called the Western Reserve, under patent to the State of Connecticut. The early settlers were a literal group; they named their outpost on the west bank "Mouth of the Black River."

It remained a sparsely settled location until John S. Reid came to the area around 1811 and began to cut down trees for roads and farmland. He was instrumental in creating a real village. Reid, his sons and his sons-in-law renamed the village Charleston in 1836 for reasons unknown and then renamed it Black River a few years later. Then, in 1874, it was decided to change the name once again. Residents voted to change the name to Lorain, after the county in which it was located.

Settled primarily by colonists from the northern states, most of northern Ohio was strongly antislavery, and Lorain was no exception. During the Civil War, the factories and mills of Lorain were key to the war effort. The town also began to be known as a grain-shipping center, and very slowly the port began to grow in importance. With such a good location on Lake Erie, it was only a matter of time before shipbuilding was recognized as a viable enterprise.

To accommodate all the commerce centered in Lorain, the Nickel Plate Railroad began to ship needed goods into the city and then shipped out the completed products for sale. The railroad decided that a drawbridge was needed to facilitate the trains. When it was completed in 1908, the

Nickel Plate drawbridge across the Black River was the longest single-span drawbridge in the world. It was an investment the Nickel Plate Railroad thought worth the effort. In the fishing industry alone, the Nickel Plate Railroad shipped out four to five million pounds of fish annually to the markets of the East Coast and west to the Great Plains states.

After taking in the sight of the train cars resting in the sludge of the Black River, many of the boys pedaled over to American Shipbuilding, where the company proudly displayed the newly constructed *Henry Ford II*, a massive oar carrier ordered by Henry Ford himself. It was still in the dry docks on June 28, 1924, awaiting a few finishing touches before being delivered to Detroit.

8:00 a.m., Lakeview Beach, Lorain

As the sun drew higher in the sky and the temperature rose, Lake Erie beckoned to swimmers, boaters and fishermen, and more and more people made plans to cool off on the lake. People worked hard during the week, and now they wanted to relax and enjoy themselves. What better way to enjoy blue sky and sun than by going to the beach? Lakeview Park, only minutes from downtown, was a big draw, especially with the new two-story bathhouse, built in 1919, where bathers could change comfortably from swimsuits to street clothes and vice versa.

Others were drawn to Lakeview Park because of the lovely view. You could enjoy a picnic lunch under the giant oaks and buckeyes and gaze out at the immense lake. To the right, far out on the peninsula, was the lighthouse, a popular landmark that captured the interest of artists and photographers.

Reflecting the popularity of the park, an energetic entrepreneur by the name of Joseph Blinzley took over the concession of the beach, making sure the bathhouse was well maintained so swimmers would be able to change in comfort and then step right out onto the sand. Joseph ran the concession along with this wife, Catherine. It was perfect employment for the middle-aged couple. Their three children were grown, and it was a lovely place to work.

By 8:00 a.m. on June 28, 1924, Joseph and Catherine Blinzley were already at the beach, opening their business for the day. Running the concession involved many tasks. They had to make sure that the beach was clean and ready for use. Garbage bins had to be dumped and the bathhouse wiped down and prepared for the new day's clientele. The beach had several food concessions run by teenagers, whom the Binzleys employed. Food had to be stocked, along with beverages. There would be a lot of cold drinks sold on a hot day like today. It was unusually still, with bright sun and high humidity. The Blinzleys probably guessed that swimmers would come out in droves.

Yes, it would be a busy beach day.

Shading her eyes from the sun, Catherine Blinzley would have looked out over the lake and seen small fishing boats dotting the skyline. It was a perfect day to be out on the water, but the few sailboats on the horizon were limp in sail. The water was fairly flat for Lake Erie. Only small, baby waves licked the shore.

Having grown up in the area, Catherine would have been aware that not many miles out was the wreck of the *Morning Star*, a passenger ship that sank on a rainy summer night in 1868, taking at least forty people to their watery grave.

But today was bright and sunny!

Lake Erie promised a delightful, if busy, day. To get to the second story that opened into the parking lot, Catherine had to climb back up the stairs. From the second story of the bathhouse, she would have been able to see her husband sweeping the parking lot. Joseph Binzley was an enterprising and hardworking man.

Pausing to catch her breath from her climb, Catherine would have looked out at Lakeview Park behind the beach. Already, people were beginning to stroll under the oak and buckeye trees, many walking their dogs and stopping to chat with friends. Over at the new tennis courts, four men were playing an early game of doubles. Her husband was right. This would be a busy day.

Lakeview Park was the brainchild of one man, Leonard Miller Moore. A former mayor of Lorain, Moore was a man of great foresight. When he was in office, it troubled him greatly that although Lorain was situated on a vast lake, there were no town beaches. In 1916, acreage that had once been part of the Gillmore Farm came up for sale. Moore badgered the city council to purchase land on the water for public use.

After much deliberation, discussion and protest, the City of Lorain purchased approximately forty acres of land for $53,551.38. Situated at 1800 West Erie Avenue, it was considered "out of town" by many people, but when Lakeview Park, with its modern bathhouse, beautiful beach, concessions, deck, picnic areas and shaded woods, was finally opened to the public, it was hailed as a great success. At its peak, the beach could accommodate more than two thousand bathers.

10:00 a.m., Lorain

In 1924, Lorain was a prosperous city with many different groups of people in its melting pot. The residential districts reflected this diversity. Along the lakeshore, large Victorian and Edwardian homes graced the boulevard leading to town. Like the lakeshore homes, in the city itself, the streets in the affluent middle-class neighborhoods were made of brick and stone and were shaded by towering buckeyes, oak trees and maples. The lawns were neat, often enclosed by iron fences, with gardens landscaping the properties.

Near the industrial area by the Nickel Plate drawbridge, the factory workers had their neighborhoods. Built close to the industries where the men found work, these much smaller homes were made of wood and close together. The neighborhoods were often defined by ethnicity: the Italian neighborhood; the Polish area; Hunkyville, where the Hungarians congregated; and so on.

The Van Deusen house on Fifth Street was in the established section of town. A successful lawyer, C.E Van Deusen owned the stately home. It was a great place to entertain guests. On Saturday, June 28, the household was bustling with preparations for the arrival of relatives driving up from Columbus. Van Deusen's two sons—Richard, age eight, and Wilbur, age three—were excited. Their three cousins, an uncle and two aunts were driving up from Columbus for the weekend. Their sister, Jean, was in Cleveland with friends. She would come home later.

Since breakfast, the children would have been demanding to know the arrival time of their guests. It would be a while, their father told them. It was over 125 miles to Columbus. Driving at a good clip of thirty or so miles an hour, it would take their relatives a good four hours to get to Lorain.

11:00 a.m., Lorain

For Ellen Meredith, age forty-five, a beach day was definitely the plan. Born and raised in Lorain, she now lived in Swissvale, Pennsylvania, with her husband but frequently took the train back to Lorain to visit her aging parents and her brothers. Her brother Harry Buttle, thirty-five, was recently divorced and back in the family home with his son, William. The day before, Ellen had boarded the train from Pittsburg to Cleveland and then headed on to Lorain, where her family picked her up at the station.

The Buttle home was within walking distance of Lakeview Park, so after a quick lunch, Ellen strolled to the beach, along with Harry and William.

They changed into their beach clothes in the new bathhouse. Harry wore the two-piece wool bathing suit of a middle-aged man, but his son probably opted for the more modern one piece. As for Ellen, it is safe to assume she was eager to get in the water. Her wool bathing dress and black stockings were exceptionally hot on such a muggy day.

All around them were familiar faces. Catherine Blinzely, who was supervising the teenagers who worked in the food and drink concessions, must have greeted them as familiar beach enthusiasts. Ellen and Harry spread out their towels and began to catch up on family news. William left them for the concession stand, which was manned by his pretty high school classmate Mary Kodelja.

As Ellen and Harry chatted, they could see that out on the lake the sailboats were now traveling at a good clip.

12:00 p.m., Lorain

By 1924, Lorain had grown from a village to a prosperous, industrial center and shipping port, drawing immigrants from all over the world. Lured by the promise of good jobs, the city's population jumped from 1,595 people in 1880 to 38,000 people in 1924, making it one of the larger Ohio cities. The cities of the north shore, especially Elyria, Cleveland and Lorain, were joined together by an intricate web of streetcars lines.

Mary Peters, a thirty-one-year-old Greek immigrant, frequently took the streetcar to Elyria to visit her brother, Spero Valassis. Spero owned a restaurant and candy shop in that city. Elyria was only eight miles away, but today's visit was cancelled. The day was simply too hot and muggy to take three little children out of the house.

Mary's husband, John Peters, had just come home from his candy shop, the Lorain Candy Kitchen. The couple lived with their children—Gus, age ten; Lucille, eight; and Theodore, five—on Fourth Street, along with two boarders who helped out at the Candy Kitchen.

As for many people from Greece, their big meal of the day was at noon. Mary would have prepared vegetables, a salad with olive oil and lemon juice dressing and some meat dish like chicken. After eating, John would have gone upstairs to take a nap before returning to work. His day started at 6:00 a.m. and ended at 10:00 p.m., so this nap was vital.

Taking care of a household of seven was always hard, but on a hot, humid summer day, it was especially trying. With her husband sleeping, Mary spent

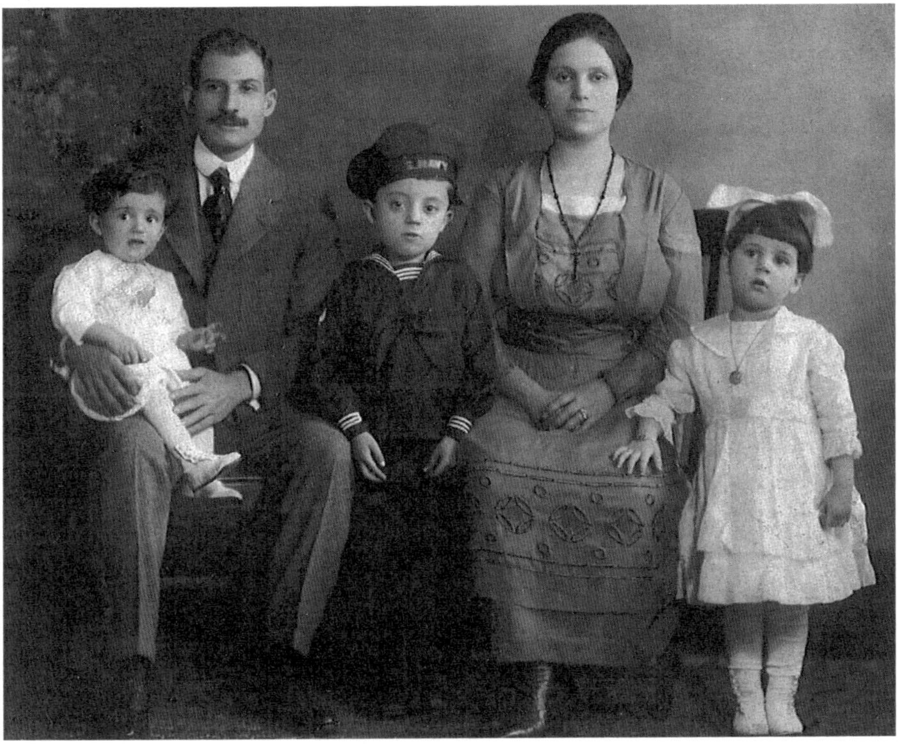

Mary and John Peters and their children. They survived the storm but moved back to Greece. *Courtesy of the Valassis Family Collection.*

the early afternoon hanging out the clothes she had washed that morning. Washing clothes—a process that involved washing them in the basement, putting each item through a ringer, lugging everything upstairs and outside and then hanging the wash out to dry in the hot sun—was laborious.

There was no time to take the children to the beach, which had been the backup plan of the day.

Another immigrant woman who had her hands full was Louis Foisy's wife, Josephine. Born in Quebec, she and her husband had moved to Lorain, where Louis found employment as a riveter at American Shipbuilding. In 1924, she was the mother of eleven children, all of whom lived at home with her and her husband in their house at 1045 G Street in the working-class area of town. It was hard to raise such a large family on a riveter's salary, but Louis was frugal and carefully saved what he could in a dresser drawer. Like many immigrants, he was not too trustful of banks.

Not too far away, at 1326 Reid Avenue, Bessie Widzer, age twelve, lived with her sister and parents. The family had emigrated from Dvinsk, Latvia, in 1912, before Bessie was born. Drawn by the prosperity of Lorain, the Widzers and their three daughters had anticipated a good life in the United States, but in 1918, their daughter Sadie died in the Spanish flu epidemic. Now it was just Bessie, her sister Mary and her parents, who kept the Jewish Sabbath. Bessie had permission from her parents to go to the State Theater for the 5:00 p.m. showing of the silent movie that was playing. The city had several theaters, but the State was the nicest.

1:00 p.m., Lorain

Mary Kodelja was a clerk at Lakeview Park. She ran a concession stand for the Blinzleys and loved her summer job. An outstandingly beautiful brunette, the sixteen-year-old drew all the handsome young men who came to swim. Along with her younger sister, Anna, she was very popular.

A summer job at Lakeview Park was fun but also a very real necessity for the two sisters. Their family needed the money the girls earned.

It was not an uncommon immigrant story. Mary's mother and father were immigrants from Yugoslavia, arriving in Lorain around 1906, hoping for a better life in the United States. Mary was born in 1909 and Anna two years later. In 1912, when Mary's mother was pregnant with her third child, Martin died, leaving his widow in dire straights. A third daughter, Sophia, was born in 1913. Mrs. Kodelja became a laundress to support her children and was still listed as a widow in the 1920 federal census. Only recently had she remarried to a fellow Yugoslavian immigrant with the last name of Zgonc.

Mary loved to be at the beach and watch the children playing in the waves. Today, the waves started out fairly flat, but they were starting to get bigger, and far out on the lake, a boater said he saw white caps forming. If she looked through her binoculars, she could see them, too.

Other beaches dotted the shore of Lake Erie, but Lakeview Park beach was one of the most popular destinations. Besides the sand and water, there was a convenient parking lot. People with automobiles could sit and take in the view. Today, the parking lot was filling up rapidly, and everyone near the water commented on the pleasant breeze.

2:00 p.m., Lorain

It was a little less comfortable at the Crystal Restaurant, located in a four-story building near the Mills Feed Store. Mary Campbell was the lone waitress on the busy day shift, working alongside the cook. The grill gave off a lot of heat, which made Mary's job even harder on such a muggy day. Mary turned up the fans in the dining room, but it did little to cool things down.

Mary didn't envy the people who lived in the upstairs apartments. The heat from the restaurant rose up through the vents to the upper stories of the building, and it became uncomfortable in the apartments above the restaurant. The LaLonde family lived on the third floor. Mr. LaLonde was a tugboat captain on Lake Erie, but his wife and three children were at home.

To catch the most breeze, Catherine LaLonde would have opened all her windows to let in any wind that might be blowing off the lake. From her position on the third floor, she was able to look out her window toward the Mills Feed Store, where Mrs. Gertrude Mills was working. Gertrude's husband was out on the lake, too, but unlike Catherine's husband, Mr. Mills wasn't working. He had gone out for some recreational fishing, and both women would probably have been looking forward to Sunday, when their husbands would be home.

2:30 p.m., Lorain

Lorain was bustling as the day moved into the afternoon hours. Because all stores were closed on Sundays, it was important to get errands done. Downtown, the sidewalks were packed with shoppers. Crossing the streets was a real challenge. Besides avoiding the busy trolley lines, pedestrians had to contend with the growing number of automobiles. It seemed like anyone who could afford a car bought one. Going for a ride was a popular activity, especially on a beautiful summer day.

Another draw in town was the State Theater, which was having a special program. Over one thousand children were spending their Saturday afternoon at the theater to watch a silent movie presentation. There would be another showing later in the day. This was the showing that Bessie Widzer planned to attend.

Mary Hirsch worked at the State Theater. It would be a busy day for a Mary, who was seated at her piano in the orchestra pit. She played the score that accompanied the silent movie. Today, the title of the accompanying music was "Sacrifice." In the windowless orchestra pit, Mary knew only that it was stifling hot, and it would be a long day.

As for Ellen Meredith, Harry Buttle, William and the other hundreds of bathers at Lakeview Park, the biggest worry was sunburn.

3:00 p.m., Sandusky

Today, when people think of Sandusky, Ohio, the first thing that comes to mind is Cedar Point, the amusement park famous for roller coasters. Covering over 364 acres, Cedar Point is located on a peninsula jutting into Lake Erie. In 1924, Cedar Point was important because it housed the ferry terminals for boats servicing the offshore islands.

The actual town of Sandusky faces Sandusky Bay and the open water of Lake Erie and has its own harbor and docks. *Sandusky* is a Wyandot Indian word for "cold water in pools." The Wyandots were one of the tribes that did business with French fur traders who moved into the area in the 1700s.

The French presence in northern Ohio diminished as England sent more and settlers to the shores of Lake Erie, and after the French and Indian War ended in 1760, the French forts, including Fort Sandoski, became British garrisons tasked with the mission of guarding British settlers. These new settlers were mainly farmers and traders, and they settled the land and stayed, gradually displacing the Indian population.

Fort Sandoski, then changed to Fort Sandusky, was deserted by the British soon after it came under their control. A new fort was built a short distance away in 1761. This new fort was burned by Indians during Pontiac's Rebellion in 1763.

Established as a city in 1818, the railroad came to Sandusky in 1835. The Mad River and Lake Erie Railroads broke ground on September 17, 1835. This led to the buildup of the city as an industrial and shipping center for both lake traffic and rail. From Sandusky Harbor, steamboats ferried passengers to the islands dotting the western waters of Lake Erie.

By the dawn of the twentieth century, Sandusky proper had continued to prosper, mainly as a transportation hub. Two railroads went through town, and the town became well known for its fisheries, harbor and wine industry. It had many small factories that kept employment up and added to the prosperity of the area.

In 1924, Sandusky boasted a population of more than twenty-six thousand people and was the unchallenged hub for north shore boat and ferry excursions to the western islands. Sandusky even boasted its own United States Weather Bureau office, which was placed strategically right on the waterfront, where the new meteorologist, C.C. Cooper, could look out over Sandusky Bay. From his office in the Weather Bureau, Cooper was also in a good position to monitor the street traffic in Sandusky. At three o'clock on the last Saturday in June 1924, shifts at the various factories had finished, and more than one thousand workers, lunch pails in hand, were hurrying home.

It was such a hot, sultry day that workers were grateful to be done. Jumping back and forth from his instruments to the window overlooking the harbor, Cooper was apprehensive. There was a low-pressure area coming east, and at about three o'clock it had started to sprinkle. His barometer was dropping quickly, and there was an ominous look to the sky, which had changed from blue to an odd shade of gray.

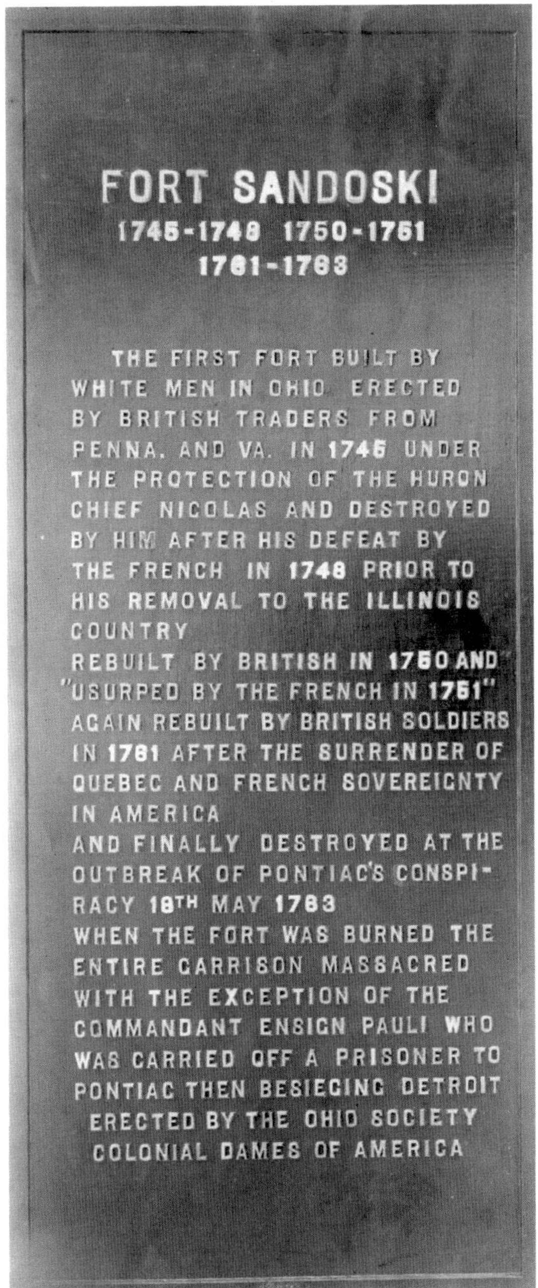

Fort Sandusky (Sandoski) Memorial. *Ohio Historical Society.*

3:45 p.m., Lorain

A sailor's wife, Catherine Lalonde often looked out the window to check conditions on the lake. Born in Germany, she had married George LaLonde, and they moved to Lorain with their children. Today, it seemed like the wind had picked up, which was a blessing. The breeze cooled the apartment, and she felt no concern about a storm.

Catherine decided to ask a friend up for dinner. Mrs. Bates ironed for a dry cleaning store nearby. It was hot and miserable work, and she would appreciate the cool breeze in the apartment; it would also be a treat for her to eat with the LaLonde family instead of downstairs in the restaurant. Soon, Catherine LaLonde, Mrs. Bates and the three LaLonde children were all happily chattering over an early supper.

4:00 p.m., Lorain

Mary Peters kissed her husband goodbye as he headed out the door to go back to work. They paused on the little porch as John Peters stopped and studied the overhead clouds. He was concerned by the heaviness in the hot air and the darkening sky. He told Mary to keep the children close—a storm might be coming. Mary thought of her clothes drying on the line and hoped he was wrong.

4:05 p.m., Sandusky

Twenty-six miles away in Sandusky, some boaters were still out, taking advantage of the summer day, but the rain was forcing many small boats to hurry back to shore and dock in the harbor.

At the Point, it had started to rain a little harder, but most hoped the squall would pass. Dressed in their summer finery, people filled the large ships that ran between Cedar Point and the offshore islands. The mood was festive, but those who were watching the sky commented on the change in color from a light blue to an odd shade of tan.

The streets of hilly Sandusky were not crowded leading down to the waterfront, but what activity there was existed mainly in the area around the docks at the harbor as men scurried to secure their boats before heading home for dinner.

United States Weather Bureau meteorologist C.C. Cooper watched the sky with growing concern. In his small office by the harbor, the meteorologist studied his instruments and made calculations. He knew the big low front coming in from the west was already colliding with the high-pressure system stuck over Lake Erie. The high-pressure system didn't want to budge, and the low-pressure system refused to stop moving east. This was a recipe for disaster as the two weather systems engaged in battle. Cooper was the first to recognize there was a serious problem developing out on the lake. Ominous clouds were forming over Sandusky Bay, and now the sky was taking on a greenish yellow tint.

4:15 p.m., Cedar Point, Sandusky

Before it was famous for its roller coasters, Cedar Point was famous for its thousands of cedar trees. The amusement park was built in 1870, making it the second oldest in the United States. The dense cedar forest covered the whole peninsula and went right down to the shore. Now the branches of the proud cedars were dancing around in the wind coming from two different directions.

The ferries heading to the islands were still taking on passengers. Some people commented on the white caps forming out on the lake, but there was little anxiety amongst the holiday crowd. But the captain of one of the largest ferries was watching the sky with growing concern. Over one thousand passengers were his responsibility, and with a storm coming, there was no room for error. With years of experience sailing on the capricious lake, the captain would have been cautious. He watched from the bridge, sensing this was no small thunderstorm.

4:20 p.m., Sandusky

The rain was now coming down in sheets, followed by hail. In the harbor, the incoming waves grew higher, and the vessels tied at the docks started to bob up and down, jerking at the ropes that kept them moored. Farther out in the harbor, more and more white caps dotted the black water. The lake was becoming rough. Meteorologist C.C. Cooper didn't envy anyone caught out on the open water during this storm.

4:25 p.m., Lakeview Park in Lorain

It wasn't the weather but the approaching dinner hour that made a few people slowly get up and call it a day at Lakeview Park. At almost four thirty that afternoon, there were approximately three hundred people still frolicking in the water or lying on the sand. There was no cause for concern. Without radios, television or any modern weather forecasting systems in place, the Saturday bathers had no idea two monster weather systems were converging to the west of them.

Noting the wind picking up, Mary Kodelja began to put bottles of ketchup on her napkins so they wouldn't blow away. It looked like it might start to rain soon. Safe inside her concession stand, she wouldn't have been concerned. Her sister, Anna, would be out of the rain in the bathhouse, so there was no worry there.

4:30 p.m., Downtown Lorain

At the State Theater, it was much hotter and muggier than at the beach. Mary Hirch, confined in the orchestra pit, was tired, and the pianist knew there was still one more show to do. Inside the theater, almost one thousand patrons were filing out, but the manager said there were at least two hundred tickets sold for the five o'clock show. Mary stood up and stretched her legs. The State Theater was a beautiful place to work, but on days like today, it took a lot of stamina to get through the double performances.

4:33 p.m., Sandusky

Perhaps there was not concern in Lorain, but twenty-five miles to the west in Sandusky, there was a frightening change in the atmosphere, and C.C. Cooper noted this in his log. Enormous, jagged bolts of lightning ripped through the black cumulous clouds over the bay. The storm was erasing the sunlight, and it seemed like it was almost night.

There was no doubt bad weather was coming, so the few people still outside hurried home to take shelter and eat their waiting dinners.

C.C. Cooper raced between his meteorological instruments and the window facing Sandusky Bay. He could see two fronts, one from the southwest and one from the northwest, at a point of collision. At that point, a bluish black cloud in rotation could be observed, but it had not touched down on the water.

The barometer was now in free fall—a very bad sign. Literally hanging out the window of his office, C.C. Cooper watched the monster thunderstorm begin to take shape. Out on Sandusky Bay, the water was frothy with waves from the rising wind. Violent flashes of lightning skewered the black, rumbling clouds.

The first two people to actually see damage from the storm were on the seventh floor of the Feik Building. Dr. J.C. Cramer and a local dentist, L.E. Meyer, shared an office with windows facing the bay. The two men gave an account of what they saw to the *Sandusky Register* newspaper:

> *The weather was queer all afternoon...we were admiring the beauty of the clouds, with lightning dashes zigzagging through the black clouds...suddenly as we watched a black square shaped cloud appeared over the bay and approached from the northwest toward the Hinde & Dauch Company building. We saw the chimney topple over...it gained a momentum and swiftly lashed toward the Cedar Point dock. We saw the roof suddenly rip off into the air just as though someone had touchd off a stick of dynamite. It all happened quicker than you could snap your finger...pieces of roof were whirling all around and we thought our windows would be blown, but*

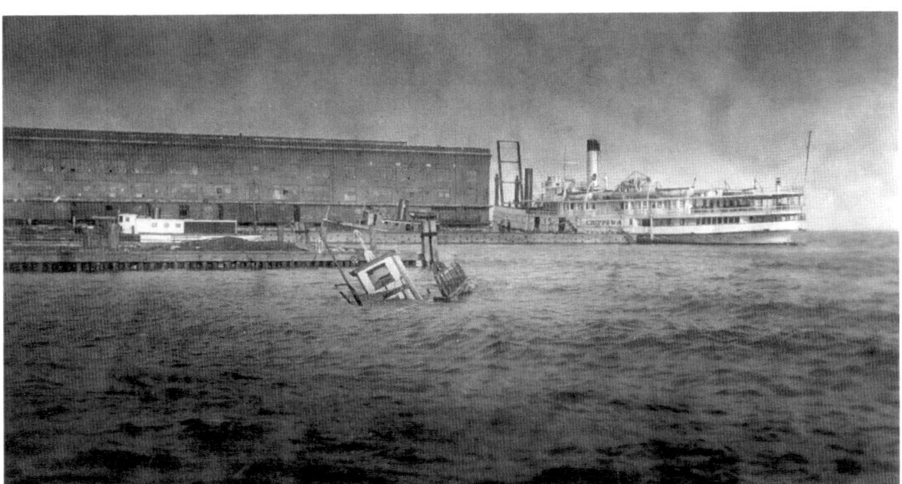

The *Chippewa* at Fort Jackson in Sandusky, Ohio. The Hinde and Dauch factory is to the left of center. *Sandusky Library Archives Research Center.*

> *just as suddenly as it had come, the wind changed and swept directly east across the water front…farther east we couldn't see because of the driving rain. It was a sight I shall never forget.*

The rotating winds begin to spin as the clouds appeared to descend closer to the angry lake. With growing horror, C.C. Cooper watched as a massive tornado began to come down from the enormous super cell created by the colliding weather systems. With terrifying rapidity, the funnel began to dance across the water. Quickly making computations, Cooper calculated the funnel's path and realized it was heading straight for the Sandusky waterfront. He glanced at his clock and rapidly jotted down the time.

It was 4:33 p.m.

The United States Weather Bureau Report, published on August 1, 1924, was concise:

> *The storm center passed about one thousand feet north of the Weather Bureau office at approximately 4:35 p.m., the barometer falling abruptly by 0.20 inch and within five minutes regaining its former height; the rain, which had been light since it started at 4:15, became heavy and so continued till 8:15, the total fall being 1.41 inches. The wind register indicated the quickest mile at the rate of seventy-seven miles per hour.*

Whipping the waves into a boiling frenzy, the violent wind assaulting the harbor registered at just under eighty miles per hour. The howling sound that ripped through the town was described by some imaginative people as approximating the manic cry of a banshee. The high-pitched shriek assaulted the ears of the people of Sandusky. For those few souls on the dock gazing north, there was little time to run to safety. The rest of the small town was oblivious to the terrible danger as people sat down to early suppers. Only the lashing rain and increasingly loud wind would have been tip-offs that an unusually bad storm was approaching.

As recorded by the United States Weather Bureau at 4:35 p.m., the tornado blasted on shore at the waterfront, tossing boats around with abandon and ripping up the wooden moorings of the dock. One thousand yards away, trapped in the small building that housed the U.S. Weather Bureau, C.C. Cooper had an on-site lesson in what an F4 tornado could do.

The waterfront was the worst hit. The suction power of the funnel yanked boats from their moorings and flung them like toys in a bathtub—either sending them back into the water or smashing them into buildings. Nearby

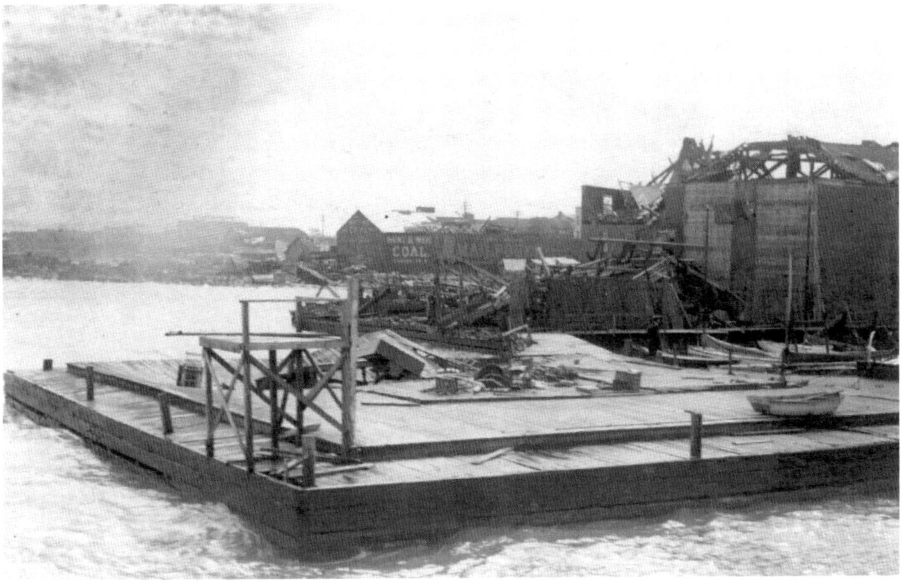

The location of the Sandusky Yacht Club after the storm. The entire clubhouse was destroyed in less than a minute. *Sandusky Library Archives Research Center.*

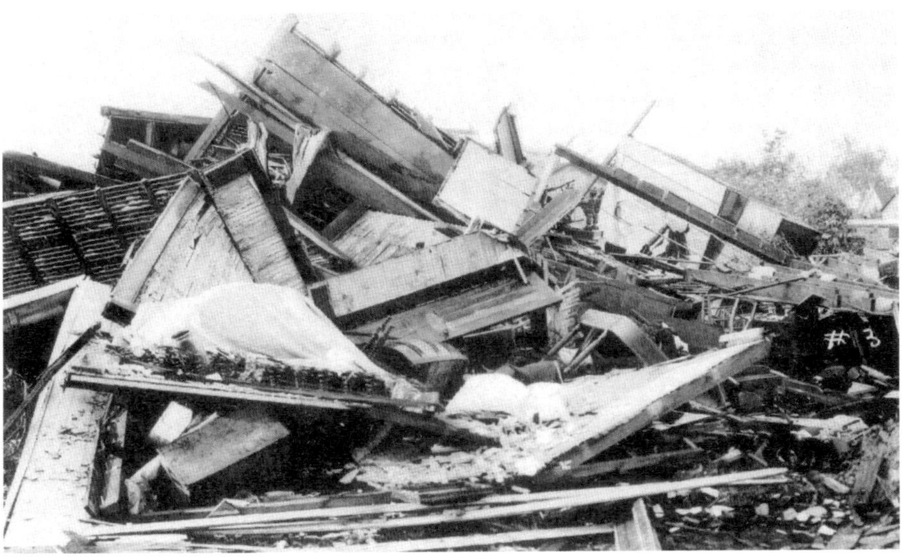

Destruction on East Market Street in Sandusky, Ohio. *Sandusky Library Archives Research Center.*

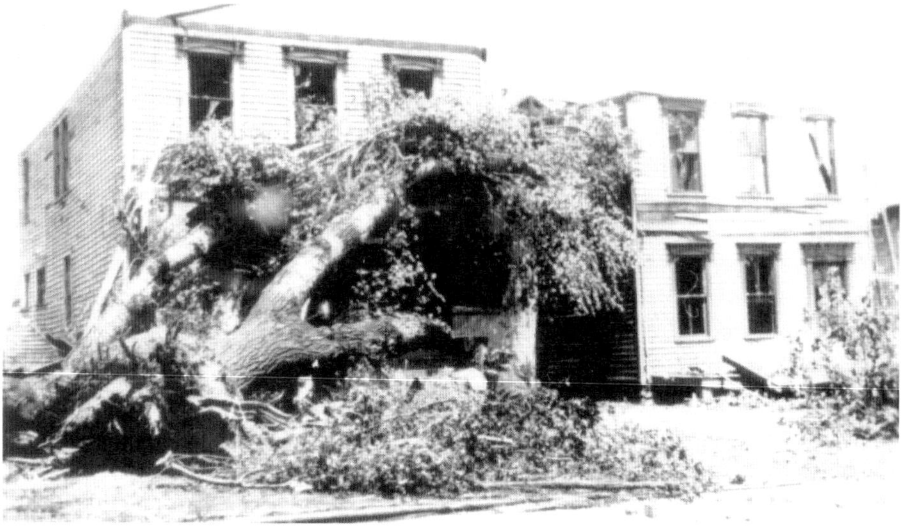

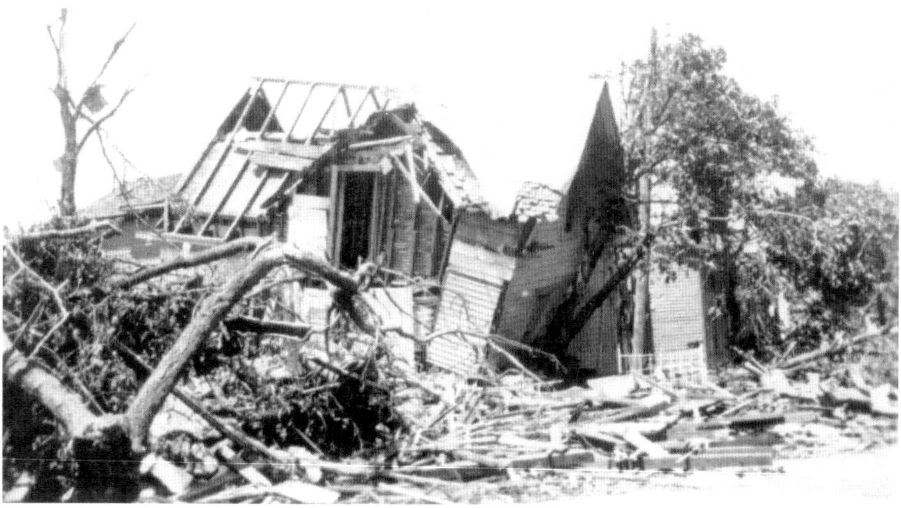

Many homes were destroyed in Sandusky. *Sandusky Library Archives Research Center.*

waterfront fisheries were destroyed. On a rampage of destruction, the winds smashed the Sandusky Yacht Club into unrecognizable pieces.

In less than five minutes, the tornado traversed an area a quarter mile wide and a little more than a half a mile long. It destroyed a nine-block section of the village bordered by Market Street, Adam Street, Washington Park and the waterfront. Mercifully, the business area of Sandusky was almost deserted because it was late Saturday afternoon.

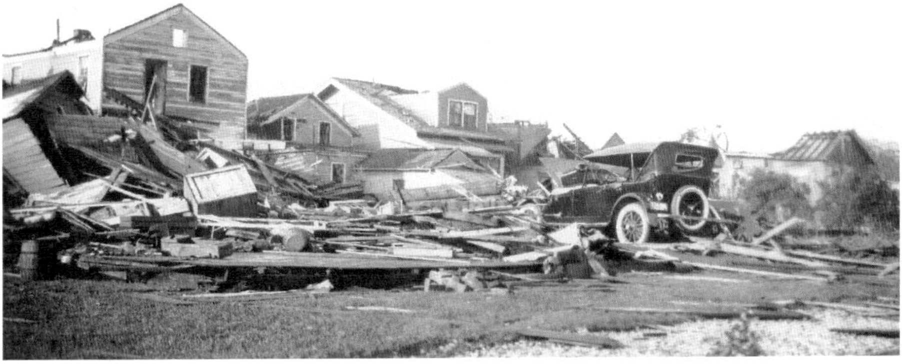

The M.R. Herb residence after the tornado struck. *Courtesy of the R.B. Hayes Presidential Center, Charles Frohman Collection.*

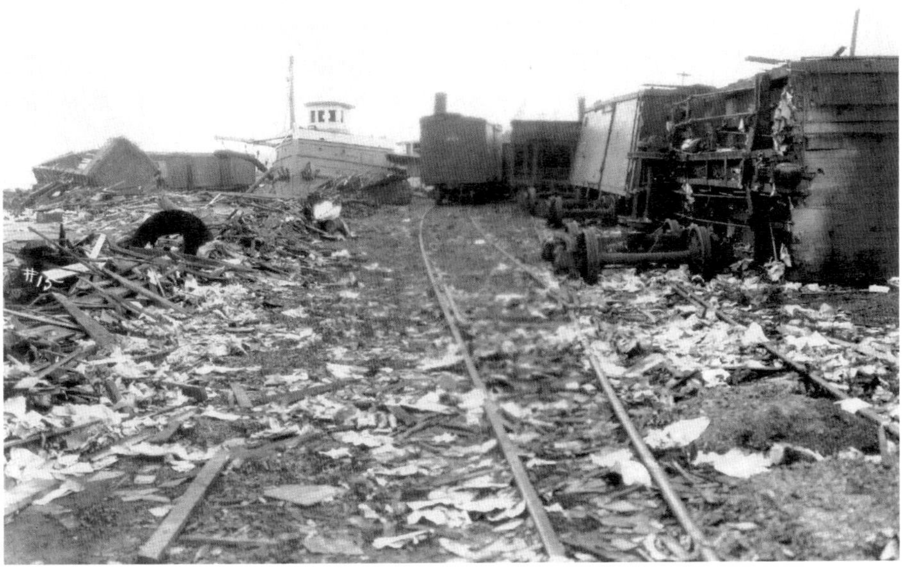

Tornado destruction in Sandusky, Ohio. *Sandusky Library Archives Research Center.*

Down by the railroad yard, the funnel sucked an office building off its foundation. When it collapsed, three people died. Farther down the street, another man was lifted into the air and hurled to his death. The tornado then hit the rail yard and lifted two train cars simultaneously into the air. Then

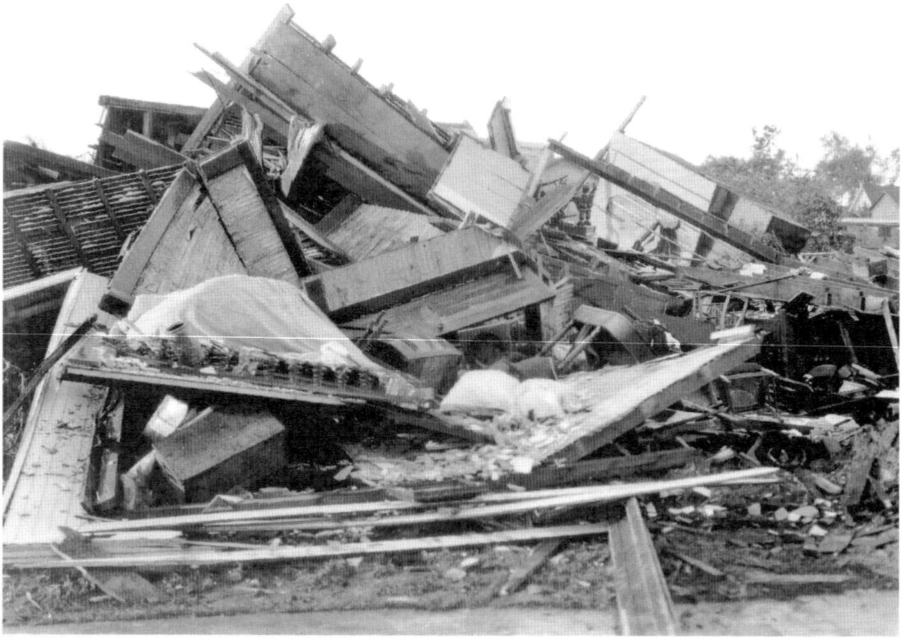

The tornado was extremely destructive at the train yard in Sandusky, Ohio. *Sandusky Library Archives Research Center.*

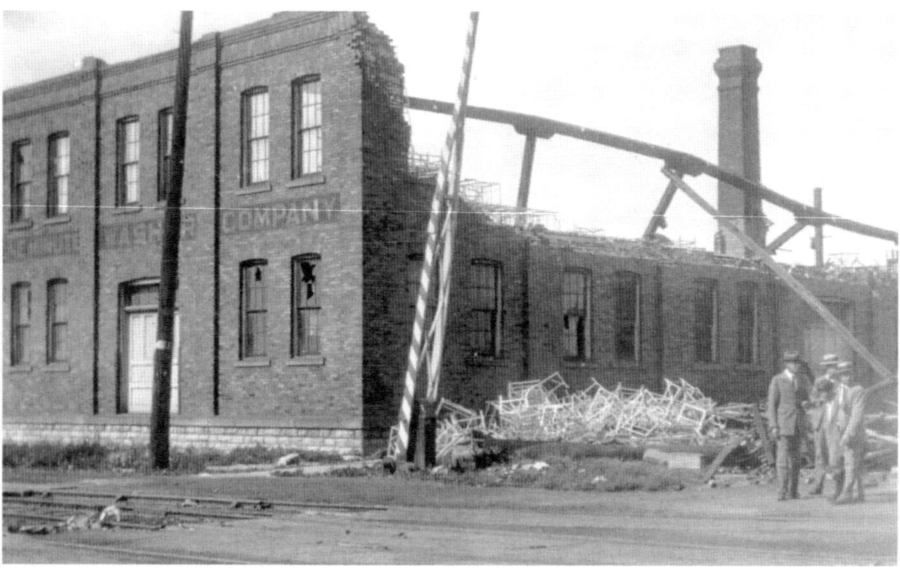

Waite Company. *Sandusky Library Archives Research Center.*

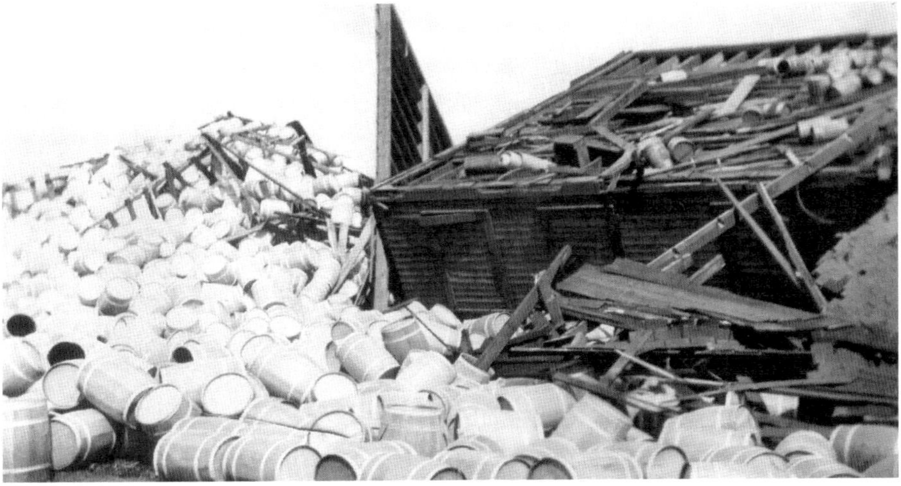

Kilburn Cooperage in Sandusky, Ohio. *Sandusky Library Archives Research Center.*

it flung the cars together like two pieces of bread in a sandwich, crushing a yard worker caught between them.

Although most factory workers had gone home, there were still people working when the tornado came barreling through the industrial area. Two people were working at the Groch Coal Company when the funnel struck it head on. The building collapsed, killing a bookkeeper and another office employee.

For the residents of the little town, there was barely any warning. The stunned occupants of the houses near the waterfront had wrongly assumed the dense, windy rain was just another summer thunderstorm. When the tornado tore through their streets, they had only seconds to react, and by then, the damage was done. In the short time the tornado ravaged their city, seven people died, one hundred were injured and more than 120 homes were damaged or destroyed. Twenty-five factories were smashed to pieces, and damage was estimated at $1 million, with another $275,000 in the rest of Sandusky County.

Slowly opening their doors, residents gazed out through sheets of rain at the wreckage. Survivors going through the crushed buildings noticed the temperature had dropped almost twenty degrees.

At the ferry mooring at Cedar Point, horrified passengers had helplessly witnessed the massive funnel descend with a vengeance on the town and prayed the monster would not veer toward them. They watched as boats docked at the harbor were lifted like toys and flung out into the bay with a

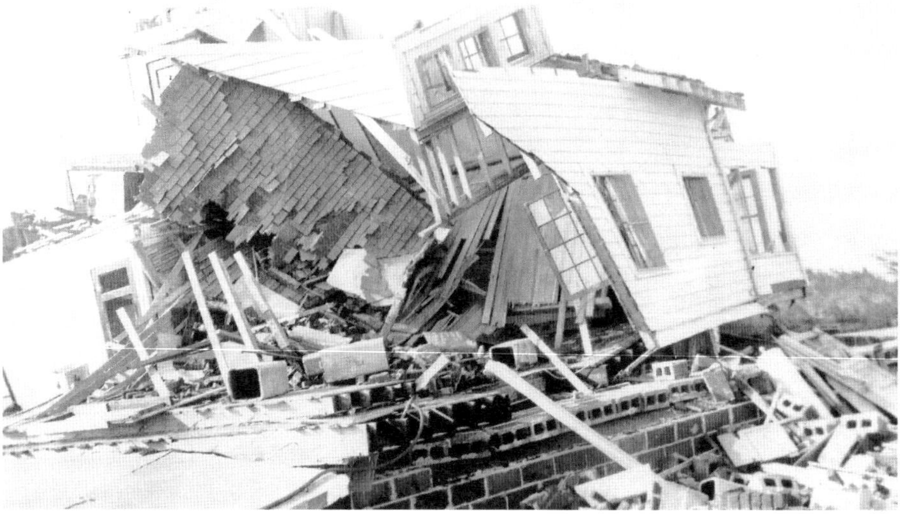

A house at the southwest corner of East Market and Meigs Streets. *Courtesy of the R.B. Hayes Presidential Center, Charles Frohman Collection.*

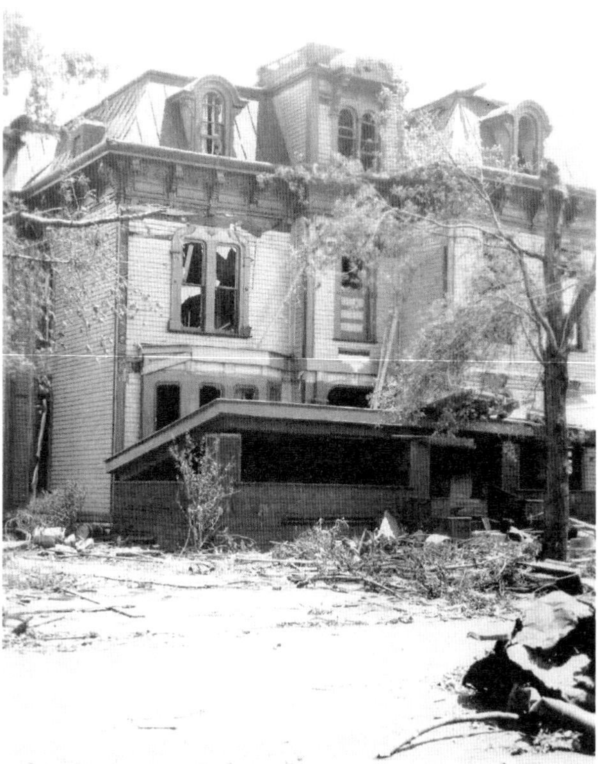

Sandusky sustained severe damage in the 1924 tornado. *Courtesy of the R.B. Hayes Presidential Center, Charles Frohman Collection.*

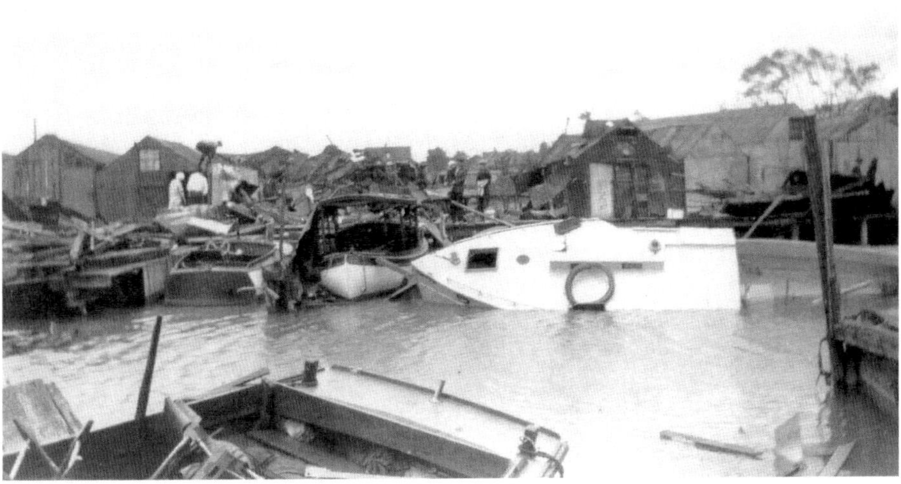

East End Cove in Sandusky, Ohio, after the tornado. *Sandusky Library Archives Research Center.*

sickening abandon that testified to the power of the storm. Many people began to pray, but all stayed in their seats, as the captain commanded them to do.

The tornado again headed for Cedar Point. In less than a minute, it mowed down a long path of cedar trees and tossed them like kindling into the woods. Then, as suddenly as it had struck the town, the twister turned backward and began to race east across the water. The nearby ferry rocked back and forth in the crashing waves, and everyone prepared for the worst. But the black funnel changed its path slightly, and the large passenger ferry with 1,200 people on board was spared.

4:45 p.m., Lake Erie

Reports from boaters out on the lake would later confirm that a massive black cloud heading rapidly east was causing storm conditions on the lake. More than one person reported that the cloud was anywhere from a mile to a mile and a half wide. High waves and gale-force winds rapidly came out of the west, shocking boaters on both small and large vessels as they struggled to stay afloat.

Those who spotted the immense black twister racing across the surface of the waves could only count their blessings when they were spared. A direct hit from this monster would have plunged their vessels down to the lake bed below, and they would have joined all the graves of earlier wrecks littering the sandy bottom of Lake Erie.

In an odd twist of fate, the storm's path edged very close to the watery grave of the coal schooner *Q.A. Gillmore*, named after General Quincy Adams Gillmore, sunk forty-three years earlier. Then the storm headed east toward Lakeview Park beach, once the Gillmore family farm.

4:50 p.m., Lake Erie

About ten miles from Lorain, a ninety-five-foot yacht named *Oswichee*, owned by J.L. Williams, ran right into the storm. Dr. M.L. Combes, a member of the Cleveland Yachting Club onboard the yacht, saw he was under an enormous black cloud flashing lightning, and then suddenly a huge funnel and a smaller waterspout descended out of the cloud. Combes and the crew fought the wild seas and bolts of lightning—and survived, even though the *Oswichee* was hit by the waterspout. The waterspout was so powerful that it sucked all the stovepipes off the vessel. Most terrifying, Combes told reporters, was the "intense darkness." Even though the ship was damaged, it eventually made it out of the direct line of the storm and found safe harbor in the port of Huron.

Combes's account is chilling: "The pressure was terrific…the water boiled and then seemed to flatten into innumerable whirlpools moving anti-clockwise."

Only twenty-six miles to the west of Sandusky, the populace of Lorain had no idea what was happening on the lake.

4:55 p.m., West of Lorain

As the storm headed east, many people in the little towns between Sandusky and Lorain observed it. People later recounted stories of high waves, wind damage and fallen branches. A Mr. Southwick, who was driving on the shore road with his family from Cleveland to Sandusky, gave one of the more vivid accounts. Four miles west of Lorain, he noticed that the weather was becoming threatening. A "dense black wall" appeared out on the lake, and the family became concerned and took shelter at the Lorain Country Club.

Mr. Southwick gave to the National Weather Service a riveting account of what they observed from the country club porch:

> *It was cone shaped, pointing downward, the cloud being 100 to 150 feet at the top end an 20 feet wide where it touched the water…the air was extremely oppressive, breathing seemed to be difficult, and noise was terrific…making a noise like a fire engine siren.*

What the Southwicks saw was the tornado heading to Lorain, four miles to the east, traveling at approximately seventy miles per hour. The tornado was gaining strength with each passing minute. And it would not continue east. Just as it reached the offshore waters of Lakeview Park beach, close to the wreck of the *Morning Star*, it would turn directly south and take dead aim for land.

4:55 p.m., Lorain

John Peters was a worried man. Having come from Greece, where the Mediterranean sun shone daily and storms were almost nonexistent, he could not get used to thunderstorms. He hated the driving rain, lightning and thunder. Now it looked like Lorain was going to have another bad thunderstorm.

John stood behind the counter of his candy store and listened as each customer walked in, talking about the coming storm. He was glad he and his staff were secure behind the heavy glass display windows facing the street, but he was worried about his wife, Mary, and their three children. Hopefully they had stayed close to home or they would be drenched.

5:00 p.m., Lorain

At five o'clock in Lorain, it was raining, humid and very hot. What was more alarming was the eerie, growing darkness over the lake, a darkness that spread over land, turning day into night. Arriving in the Lorain vicinity a few minutes after 5:00 p.m., the tornado, as if it were taking direct aim, veered south. Directly in its path was Lakeview Park beach. As if heralding the arrival of the killer storm, the black sky ripped open with wide, flashing yellow bands of lightning.

As in Sandusky, most people assumed the storm was an offshore event and would pass them by. On the beach, people slowly began to pick up their belongings before heading to the bathhouse. Thunderstorms were common events in the summer, and people were not alarmed. More important to most people was the approaching dinner hour.

In town, many people were shocked at the sudden darkness and sheets of rain driven by a wild, almost horizontal wind. Folks ducked into restaurants and stores for shelter. At the State Theater, patrons for the five o'clock show were being hurried into the lobby to escape the rain. The box office informed the manager that approximately 250 tickets had been sold for the late performance. The early performance had brought over 1,000 young people to the theater. The early show had ended at about 4:30 p.m., and everybody quickly exited the theater.

After a brief break, Mary Hirch would have sat back down at her piano in the orchestra pit, starting to play the opening stanzas of "Sacrifice." This would be the first song of the silent movie. In the windowless theater, she could not see the worsening weather, but later, she would testify that the manager told her a good storm was brewing and that he was going to start ushering patrons, mostly children and teenagers, inside the theater a bit earlier than usual.

5:05 p.m., Lakeview Park Beach

Back at the Lakeview Park beach, some people scurried for shelter, but not many were particularly worried. Others, already snug in their cars, opted to watch the storm from the parking lot, which afforded a wonderful view of Lake Erie and the Lorain lighthouse peninsula. Behind the parking lot was a lovely park where some people lingered, escaping the rain by sitting under the sheltering branches of the huge trees.

Suddenly, an alert young lifeguard peering out at the angry waves spotted a funnel beginning to descend from the underbelly of the tumultuous storm in the horizon. What was worse, it seemed to be heading their way.

He jumped from the lifeguard station and began to run up and down the sand with his megaphone and whistle, trying to get the crowd's attention. Desperately, he shouted frantic warnings to the swimmers still in the water, waving for them to come ashore, and to the stragglers still lolling on the sand.

His shouts galvanized the crowd into action. Some people, still in their bathing suits, started the race for home, while others ran to the perceived shelter of cars and nearby houses. The majority decided to take shelter in the new bathhouse, built in 1919. The concrete, two-story structure looked solid and safe. The basement, which actually opened right out onto the beach, was made of reinforced concrete. The second, or ground floor, was more exposed to the elements.

Ellen Meredith; her brother, Harry; and his son, William, were three people who raced to take cover in the bathhouse. The beach area was suddenly filled with the cries of frightened children and shouts of parents urging their offspring to run for shelter. There were two floors, and Ellen Meredith raced to the upper level, followed by William. Harry, less nimble, entered the lower section.

The tornado struck at 5:08 p.m.

Under a sinister black sky, the massive, F4 tornado careened ashore and obliterated everything in its path. Pounding rain and huge waves accompanied the funnel as it smashed sand and water on fleeing bathers. The funnel passed directly over the jammed bathhouse, sucking the first-floor structure, people and all, up into its vortex.

Howard Haupt was getting a drink at the pop stand and chatting with Mary Kodelja when suddenly the tornado sucked up the stand with Mary trapped inside. He had the strength to grab some tall grass and stay on the ground, but he later said he had felt an agonizing pain in his leg

As the pressure shifted, the bathhouse structure crashed back down into a mass of smashed and crushed concrete rubble, much of which ended up in the basement level. Everyone who had chosen shelter within the bathhouse was buried in the debris. The upper level sustained the worst of the destructive damage. The lower level offered a little more protection to those cowering within. The building was reduced to rubble except for one marble arch.

Anna Kodelja crawled out of the ruins, badly injured, and looked for her sister Mary's concession stand. It was gone. Only high grass blew in the wind where it had stood. She began to moan, both from the pain of her injuries and out of fear for her older sister.

On June 30, the *Elyria Chronicle Telegram* would recount how an unnamed lifeguard, perhaps the one who had sounded the initial alarm, was blown fifty feet back onto the sand by the storm. Pulling himself up, he watched as four people panicked and ran straight down to the water and jumped in. He pulled all of them to safety before a small tidal wave hit the beach. The undertow from the storm would have pulled them out into the lake and most certainly to their deaths.

One person bobbing in the waves was Mary Kodelja. Sucked up with her concession stand by the power of the funnel, the teenager had been dropped far out into the raging lake.

After hitting the bathhouse, the tornado careened across the parking lot and sucked up cars and fleeing people. Some were dropped back down from high above; others were blown into the water, where, if not dead already, they drowned in the now turbulent Lake Erie.

Toletha Bonsor and William Smith were sitting in his car in the parking lot when the tornado came ashore. Before they could react, their car was lifted from the ground. The Model T flew across the sand and over the water until it dropped into the churning, storm-tossed waves. Smith managed to save Bonsor and himself, but many others who were sucked up and dropped into Lake Erie were not so lucky. As Bonsor and Smith swam toward the beach, they could see other cars much farther out in the water. The fate of the occupants of those cars was grim.

Within seconds, Lakeview Park itself was decimated. Where only moments before there had been a large city park filled with oaks, maples and buckeyes, there was now only empty space. The proud trees of the park were just kindling on the ground. Every tree was knocked down, but the tennis courts, with their fragile nets, still stood upright. Except for the intact tennis courts, it was as if a bomb had gone off and destroyed the park in seconds.

When it came ashore, the funnel of the tornado was about five hundred feet across, but with terrifying power the base began to expand as it moved toward Lorain proper. The tornado proceeded to suck up or mow down every house in its path along the shore. The large Victorian homes, which had proudly stood near the water, were smashed to pieces by the wind or lifted from their foundations and dropped into the water, joining the cars and bodies of the dead now bobbing in the pounding surf.

5:09 p.m., Lorain

Within several minutes, the massive funnel was in Lorain proper. Especially hard hit were Fifth and Sixth Streets. The force of the suction and wind was enough to bend iron posts almost in half. Survivors would later tell of the terrible sound of the wind and the piercing scream of the tornado as it passed nearby. Others would remember the sound of shattering glass and the cracking of tree branches, along with the appalling thuds of trees falling to the earth. The path of the tornado was later determined to have varied from five hundred feet to four thousand feet, although it is hard to say with accuracy.

People who survived the storm later reported that day turned to night as the wind bent large trees in a way nature never intended. One entire house was lifted off its foundation and dropped a half mile away. Most houses that were sucked up simply fell apart into heaps of rubble.

Other survivors later reported that the force of the wind lifted people up and carried them away, along with a mix of flying chairs, lawnmowers, rakes and iron fences. Added to the horrible, flying montage were poor, terrified animals and domesticated fowl. Everything, living or man made, was helpless in the face of the hurricane-strength wind.

In the spacious Van Deusen home at 1128 Fifth Street, the family was preparing to sit down to dinner. It was a celebratory evening because their family guests had just arrived from Columbus. There would be ten for dinner tonight: C.E. Van Deusen; his wife and two sons; his sister-in-law, Grace Richards, and her husband, Ray; and the Richardses' three children, Leonard, Lois and Margaret. Another sister was among the guests.

As little Richard tried to close a basement door that was flapping in the wind, C.E. Van Deusen realized something was terribly wrong as the gale-force wind outside began to strengthen. Having been through another tornado, he rushed his family and the guests to the basement. This was standard operating procedure, as the basement was considered the safest spot in a tornado. Only young Margaret Richards didn't make it to the basement. Instead, the terrified eight-year-old hid near a piano in the dining room.

The anxious group in the basement, including the young children, pressed against the stairwell wall, listening as the tornado roared like a freight train overhead. To add to sounds of the wind, there was another frightening sound—a horrible creaking reverberation. It was the sound of a large house being lifted inches off its foundation and pushed sideways by one-hundred-mile-per-hour winds.

The suction and wind of the tornado were merciless. As the huge home began to shift, tons of debris fell down into the basement and on top of those seeking shelter below.

Back on Fourth Street, Mary Peters huddled with her children, listening to a dreadful din enveloping her home. Like her husband, she had been raised in Greece and was not used to storms. She waited for her husband to come home, but her fear grew with every passing second. Looking out the front window facing north, she could see that the sky had turned a bluish black.

She would later describe it as a dreadful bruise on the horizon. Around the blackness, there were odd streaks of yellow.

Out on Fourth Street, the loose objects were flying down the street, and trees were bending sideways before snapping in half. Mary raced to the window facing the backyard and saw her carefully hung clothes and towels flying off the clothesline. For one moment, she debated running out to try and save her laundry, but suddenly a metal sign, almost horizontal in the wind, flew past, pinioning a towel like a spear as it crossed the lawn.

Mary abandoned any idea of going outside and returned to her frightened children. Rain was now coming down in sheets. One of her boarders raced into the house and told her to run to the basement. She gathered her children and fled down the cellar steps as the boarder disappeared outside. It sounded as if a freight train was roaring their way. Mary began to whisper in Greek all the prayers of her Greek Orthodox faith.

Mary couldn't know it, but the base of the tornado was slowly growing like an expanding vacuum cleaner as it crossed Lorain. It had demolished Lakeview Park, the shoreline homes and the west end of Lorain.

5:10 p.m., Lorain

Having done its worst on Fifth and Sixth Streets, the twister headed for town.

The tornado hit Broadway, the main thoroughfare, at about ten minutes past five o'clock. The bottom part of the twister dragged along the street, mowing down every person, car, animal, trolley or building in its path. In seconds, tall buildings were shattered into kindling by the force of the wind. Trapped inside their homes or places of work, people were flung around at the mercy of the tornado.

Automobiles—the great new invention of the twentieth century—were just toys to this killer. Either sucked up by the funnel or blown wildly by the wind, cars in downtown Lorain became playthings in the tornado's path. Helter-skelter they were tossed into Lake Erie or blown into buildings as high as four stories and then dropped down in a crash of metal. Others blew like tumbleweed down the streets, were flipped upside down or were tossed into trees. Along with the cars, the streetcars were ripped up and tossed around, further clogging the road.

Automobiles lucky enough to stay earthbound were still damaged as they careened, out of control, down the rubble-filled streets. Another hazard was shattering glass from the buildings being destroyed. One woman told of how glass from a large building caved in the roof of her car and slashed through her legs.

The massive tornado lifted one automobile and deposited it in a tree, and another was plunged into the glass front of a store. Later, Patrolman Frank Lenham would tell of how he saw a Ford roadster picked up by the wind and dumped onto the roof of the State Theater.

The tornado was indiscriminate. People on the sidewalk looked on in horror as it approached—a massive black funnel surrounded by whirling debris. Some were killed, many were injured and a lucky few escaped. Others were lifted up into the vortex of the tornado and then dropped into the lake.

Very few buildings escaped. Business after business was destroyed.

At the Lorain Candy Kitchen, John Peters and his staff huddled in the walk-in cooler. They had fled there for safety when the front windows made of plate glass shattered inward. Seeking shelter with them were several customers, including a mother and her five-year-old son. John gave the frightened little boy a large lollipop to keep him from crying as the child's mother pulled out a rosary and began to pray. John and the others prayed for their loved ones, too.

Inside the State Theater, the patrons were oblivious. Mary Hirsch, for the second time that day, was sitting in the orchestra pit, pounding out the notes of the opening score for the movie. Bessie Widzer and her friend, sitting with about seventy-five other patrons, mostly children and teenagers, were waiting for the silent movie to start.

The music floating from the orchestra pit was the opening notes of "Sacrifice."

Everyone would have been anticipating the entertainment to come, but over the sound of the piano, the patrons began to hear something akin to a train approaching rapidly. Peering around in confusion, their ears were assaulted by a terrible shattering noise. Unbeknownst to them, the tornado had reached the eight-story Wickens Furniture Store building next to the State Theater. The ferocious winds destroyed the top of the building. The Wickens building's roof and the massive steel beams that supported the structure were ripped off and tossed onto the State Theater.

There was a sudden shaking of the State as the weight of the Wickens debris falling on its roof was too heavy to be supported. The State roof began to collapse into the fourth floor and then the third, like an accordion. Suddenly, before the ceiling caved in on the patrons, the back wall of the theater began to crumble.

Mary Hirsch stopped playing with the realization that something was terribly wrong. She leaped out of the orchestra pit and raced for the lobby, followed by much of the audience. If she had looked over her shoulder, she would have witnessed the ornate balconies of the theater begin to crash into the orchestra pit. Patrons still trapped in the theater would have disappeared under the onslaught of bricks, steel beams and concrete.

Apartments on the second, third and fourth floors began to crumble one on top of one another. Slowly, like in a bad dream, patrons in the theater began to see furniture and screaming people crash down through the ceiling on top of them. One witness later said he saw a bathtub come hurling through the roof of the lobby. Bathtubs at this time were made of cast iron, so anyone caught below this tub would surely have been grievously injured, if not killed outright.

The storm moved too fast for everyone to escape. Many people, mostly teenagers, including Bessie Widzer, were trapped in the main part of the theater. Within a minute, the roof and all four floors of the building above them collapsed, plunging them, injured and dead, into the basement hole below.

Outside the theater, the vehicle that had been thrown on the State Theater roof fell four stories to the ground just as the entire theater began to collapse, floor by floor. It joined the wreckage of the overturned trolley cars and automobiles.

The funnel continued down Broadway in a mindless path of destruction. The twister then demolished two restaurants. The Dinery was destroyed, and all who were sheltered within were killed. When it hit the building housing the Crystal Restaurant, four of the diners and a cook managed to escape. Mary Campbell, the waitress, and two other patrons were unable to escape the upper floors of the building as they plunged into the restaurant. Trapped in the doomed restaurant, they would have looked up to see the ceiling shatter and the second floor come crashing down in a cloud of choking dust.

The LaLonde family and their guest, Mrs. Barnes, were unable to flee the doomed building. Escape was impossible when the suction of the tornado made it too difficult to open the door to their apartment. Helplessly, they felt the building shudder and shake as support beams and wood shattered and the floor disappeared beneath their feet. Screaming, they tumbled to the first floor. When they finally landed in the restaurant rubble below them, there was silence. Everyone was injured or dead. An icebox landed on Catherine LaLonde, and her children were buried in the debris.

In the Mills Feed Store down the street, Gertrude Mills was running the business. No one knows if she saw the twister hit the Crystal Restaurant building, but it is almost certain that she would have heard the monster tornado racing toward her. She hid behind the counter as the store exploded into rubble. Tons of feed supplies whirled in the vortex of the funnel before crashing down on Gertrude, crushing and burying her at the same time.

The twister now headed for the Black River and the industrial area of Lorain. It hit the B&O Bridge, which spanned the river, and twisted the metal into unusable pieces. Later photographs would show the bridge resembling a roller coaster of misshapen metal.

With an expanding base, the tornado hit the American Shipyard a moment later, causing severe damage. Witnesses said that tiles began to fly off the roof of the buildings. An employee, Joseph Michalek, age thirty-three, tried to close a large freight door and was sucked out of the building, then dropped, simultaneously with a falling smokestack, to the ground below. His wife and five children were all at home.

The largest ore carrier on the great lakes, the newly built *Henry Ford II*, owned by Henry Ford, was anchored in the Black River next to the American Shipyard. The force of the storm lifted it off its moorings. The ship broke free and crashed into the unlucky Nickel Plate drawbridge, the site of the morning accident with the train. Now the ship blocked access to the city from the bridge. Farther along, at the rail yards, seventy-two locomotive cars were blown off the tracks by the force of the wind. An ice truck joined the airborne flotilla of cars and was smashed, a block away, into the window of a business.

Near the shipyard, Louis Foisy watched in horror as the huge black funnel approached. He screamed to his wife and eleven children to run to the cellar for safety. They all rattled down the stairs, terrified. Satisfied he had saved his family, Louis suddenly headed for the stairs.

"Where are you going?" screamed his wife, Josephine.

"I have to get my money and jewelry. I will be back." And he raced upstairs for his life savings.

Huddled in the basement, his family prayed he would return quickly, but the voluminous crashing of wood and bricks interrupted their prayers. Looking up, they saw nothing but sky. The house was gone, along with Louis Foisy, all sucked up in just seconds.

5:11 p.m., Lorain

From touchdown at the bathhouse until the tornado skipped back over the lake was about five minutes. Carrying a massive load of debris in its funnel, the twister headed east. It touched down in Portage and Trumbull

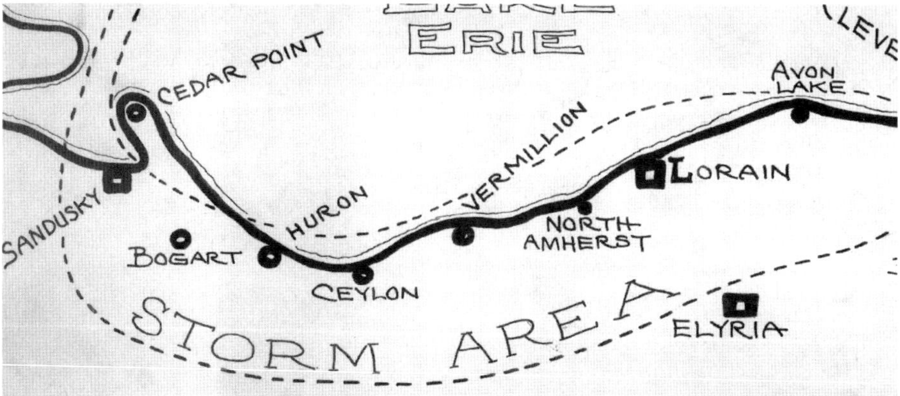

Map of the tornado destruction. *The Cleveland Press Collection, Michael Schwartz Library, Cleveland State University.*

Counties, creating a half-mile-wide path of destruction. This was an area that abounded in orchards, and hundreds, if not thousands, of fruit trees were uprooted.

It bounced overland and hit three new targets—three separate barns, miles from one another, each containing farmers milking their cows. Five thirty was milking time, and the funnel struck each barn with a vengeance, hurled humans and livestock into the air and destroyed the wooden structures. Stanley Ferry, William Herbert and Henry Lorenz were all killed when the funnel touched down at their individual farms near Mantua, Portage County, Ohio. All three farmers and all their livestock perished in the twister.

5:20 p.m., Lorain

A tornado is a very loud event. It does not whisper; it shrieks. Those who have experienced a tornado describe the sound of a train coming at you. Others tell of an unearthly howling that wipes out all other sounds—the ear-splitting shriek as the fury of Mother Nature at her worst is unleashed.

But in the moments after the tornado passed, it was eerily quiet.

Dazed and bewildered, people slowly crawled out of the rubble and looked around in shocked horror. Everything familiar was gone. All was in ruins—buildings smashed, wires down, trees uprooted, cars flung like toys into buildings or dangling from trees, the ghostly remains of once proud houses held up, if lucky, by a beam or two. Where once there had been a prosperous, modern city, the survivors saw nothing but shattered wood, uprooted trees and twisted bodies. Smashed furniture, intended to be inside houses, now sat upside down on lawns. Thousands of bricks littered the streets, and broken glass was everywhere. Walking on these terrible shards would seriously injure many people.

Their world was gone in less than ten minutes.

The destruction left by the tornado was almost incomprehensible to those who survived. Washington Avenue appeared as if a giant mower had come down the street, taking down house after house. The streets off Washington were the same. The Congregational church on Washington was caved in, its roof gone.

Broadway, the anchor of the business district, was in even worse shape. Buildings were blown in, the Masonic Temple was destroyed and cars stood one on top of the other, some even thrust by the wind into storefronts. Streetcars lay on their sides. Under the bricks and shattered glass, some people lay mercifully unconscious. Every telephone pole and electric light pole was down. Wires covered the street, but the power was off, so there no chance of electrocution or fire.

The anesthesia of shock, and the accompanying silence, lasted for only a moment. And then the groans and screams of the injured and terrified survivors began to reverberate through the air.

Twisted, broken bodies were everywhere. Some were dead, and many more were injured. One was a young boy whose mother and sister were trapped under rubble in the basement of what had been their house. The boy was crouching on the first floor when the funnel smashed the house to pieces and deposited him in the middle of the street with a broken leg. Frantically, he told rescuers that his mother and sister were in the house, not comprehending that the house was now just a pile of splintered wood. Miraculously, his sister and mother, though badly injured, survived, as did the young boy.

John Peters and his staff and customers opened the door of the cooler and walked into what was left of the Lorain Candy Kitchen. The sight that met their eyes was unbelievable. The heavy plate-glass windows were shattered, and glass was everywhere. The furniture still inside was overturned and smashed. John could see some of his chairs and tables out on the street. The candy cases were still intact, and the ice cream cooler was still standing, but that was about all that was left of his business. Edging carefully to the empty windows, John Peters looked out with disbelief at what had been a bustling business district. Now it resembled Armageddon.

The first people to crawl out of the rubble of the State Theater were a brother and sister, Dorothy Sheppard, age fourteen, and her five-year-old brother, Merlin (Buddy). Covered in plaster dust, they fled the theater and escaped the barrage of bricks and falling furniture from above. Driven by adrenaline, the little children rushed down the wind-damaged sidewalk looking like two little ghosts, until Dorothy finally collapsed from shock. Her brother stood with her until rescuers took them home to their parents.

5:27 p.m., Lorain

The outdoor clock stood on the corner of Erie and Broadway. It was a marker for many people in town. Plans to meet for shopping or dinner were followed by: "I'll meet you at the clock."

In a macabre salute to the killer storm, the clock still hung from its support trappings. The glass cover was entirely gone, and the metal hands of the clock were stopped at twenty-seven minutes past five o'clock.

6:00 p.m., the Roads to Elyria and Cleveland

Slowly, the city officials of Lorain who were uninjured began to assess the damage, and it didn't look good. The electric trolleys to neighboring towns were smashed, the tracks lifted and twisted into pieces of useless metal. Phone lines and the electric grid were also down. Trees blocked many of the streets, preventing rescuers from driving to get help. All the major bridges were twisted wrecks. Mayor George Hoffman and the city council debated how to get word out to the world about the calamity they had just endured.

The bicycle boys stepped up to the plate.

Often used as messengers, these hardy teenagers now mounted their bikes and headed south to Elyria and east to Cleveland. Others were sent out to the small farming communities nearby to alert people about what had happened. Their words were met with shocked disbelief. It was rumored that hundreds of people were buried in the State Theater collapse.

The bicycle boys who pedaled down to the lake had an even more terrible tale to tell. Where stately homes had once proudly stood by the shore, there was nothing but shattered buildings and uprooted trees. Some trees were thrust upside down like toothpicks skewering the remains of ruined homes.

The lake itself, so inviting and blue earlier in the day, was now a frothy gray debris field of turbulence. Each wave washed in pieces of houses, broken furniture, branches from trees and, unfortunately, some lifeless bodies. Far out on the water, survivors told of seeing overturned cars bobbing like corks in the angry water. The fates of the occupants were unknown. Witnesses later said they saw cars blown 150 to 200 feet out on the lake. The water was too rough to go out to try and rescue any survivors.

The moans coming from the pile of concrete that had once been the new two-story bathhouse were piteous. Sucked up by the twister, the building had then been dropped back down atop the first story. Survivors, no matter the state of their injuries, were covered with bits of smashed concrete. Those who were the least injured still suffered severe abrasions.

Already dazed and confused, the people around the bathhouse looked otherworldly from the white dust embedded in their skin. They moved slowly, pulling the wounded and the dead from the ruins. Soon, there were so many injured lying on the beach that rescuers were at a loss about how to convey them to the hospital. One person showed up in a car and began to pile some of the injured into the backseat and the trunk in a desperate effort to help.

Some of the least injured victims began to crawl out from the debris on their own. Anna Kodelja crawled all over the beach on her hands and knees in search of her sister. Harry Huapt lay stunned under what had been the concession stand. His leg was broken, and he couldn't move.

As the rescue work continued, they began to find the bodies. Ellen Meredith was found crushed to death under concrete blocks. Nearby was the body of her nephew William Buttle.

Harry Buttle was injured but alive. He crawled out of the rubble and, numb with shock, ran to his parents' home on Brownell Avenue. When he got there, the house was in ruins, but his parents had survived the storm. Harry collapsed on the front lawn, gravely injured. It is unclear whether he knew that his sister and eldest son, William, had died at the beach.

A tornado is a capricious killer.

The Van Deusen home was the scene of arbitrary destruction. The large, soundly built home had been lifted off its foundation and shifted sideways. Now the upper stories sat tilted precariously. The first floor had collapsed into the basement, where nine people huddled for shelter against a stair wall.

Nearly half of them were dead.

Grace and Ray Richards and their two children, Leonard and Lois, were killed by falling debris. Along with their bodies was little Wilbur Van Deusen, age three, also dead, in the arms of his aunt, who was only mildly injured.

Van Deusen and his wife were both injured, and their son Richard suffered a broken leg. But whether living or dead, every person in the basement was trapped in the ruins of the house, unable to escape.

The only person in the house unscathed was Margaret Richards, who had hidden in the dining room. Now the little girl sat on the porch crying for help, but no one stopped. Everyone was trying to assess their own situations, and the living Van Deusens, alone in their basement with five bodies, were trapped.

This senseless, random destruction was the same with automobiles. More than two hundred automobiles were destroyed by the tornado. So arbitrarily did the tornado pick up and fling automobiles that one young couple, Willie Cahl, and his future wife, Emma, found their car in a totally different location from where they had left it, keys still inside and still in good working order. They climbed in and drove away, astonished but happy to be safe.

Others were not so lucky. Cars were not the only things hanging from trees. People unlucky enough to be outside when the twister hit met many strange fates. One man was found hanging in a tree with two broken arms. Earlier in the day, he had been celebrating the birth of his first child. Rescuers worked for hours to get the injured man out of the tree.

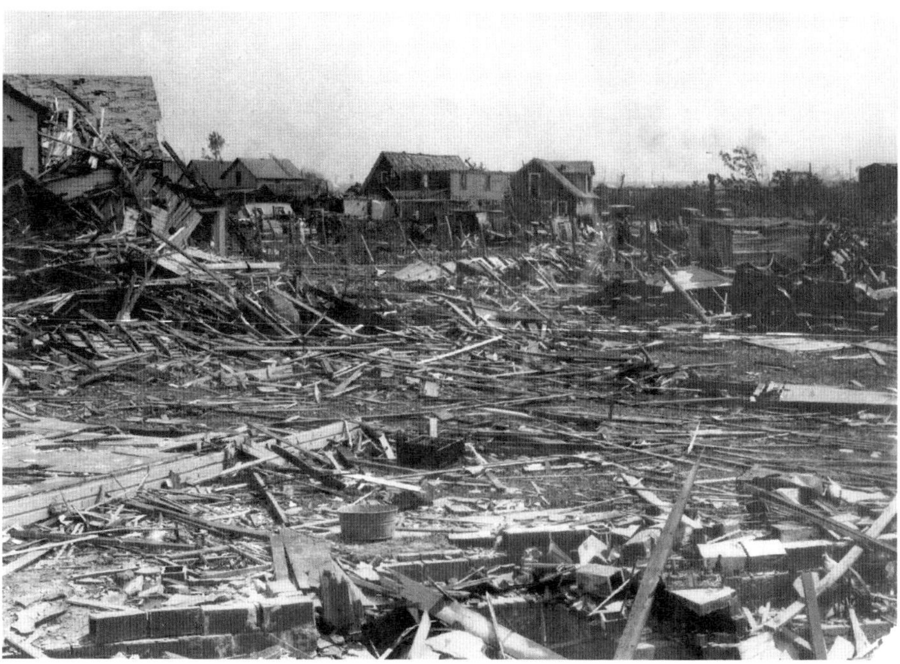

The residential district in Lorain sustained terrible destruction. *The Cleveland Press Collection, Michael Schwartz Library, Cleveland State University.*

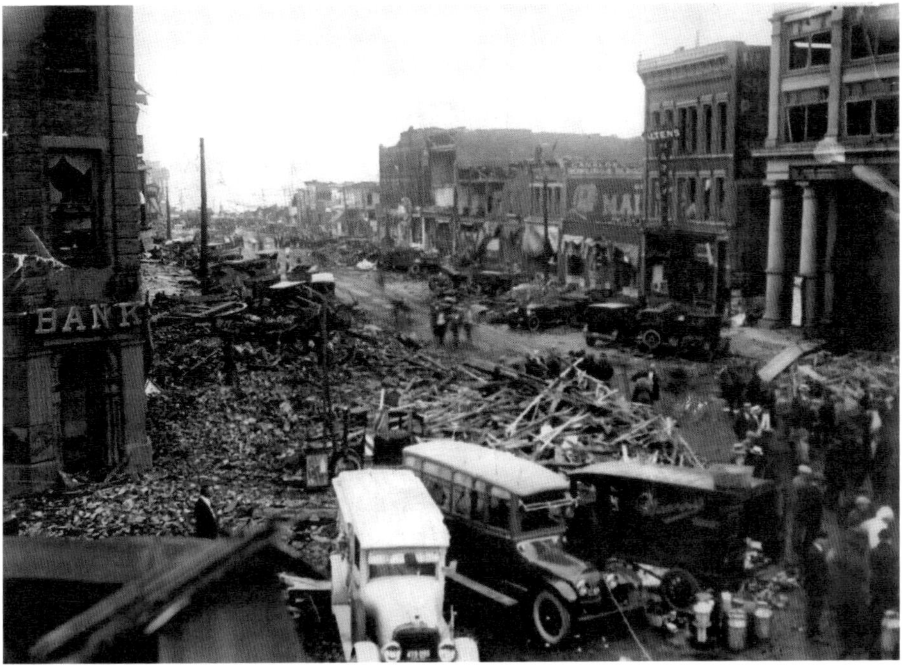

Tornado destruction in Lorain. *The Cleveland Press Collection, Michael Schwartz Library, Cleveland State University.*

On some streets, the piles of trees and branches measured fifteen to twenty feet high. To access the street, one had to crawl and climb over tree limbs and fallen wires. Yawning, open basements of what had once been houses followed one after the other. Huge piles of rubble were the final depositories of many beloved homes. In the stricken part of the city, the sidewalks were impassible.

People who had survived and were able to walk wandered through the town, dragging or carrying children. In their arms, they often held some household item. Still in shock, there was a somber air about the wanderers, as if they were sleepwalking. In truth, they were trying to identify what only an hour ago had been familiar terrain and now was a mass of destruction.

Many of the chicken coops in the city had blown away, but the birds, for the most part, survived. Now the homeless fowl pecked and clucked their way around looking for yards that had vanished along with the homes to which they had been attached. Along with the distressed fowl, one could hear the bewildered and frightened cries of dogs and cats searching for lost owners.

7:00 p.m., Elyria

The ham radio operator on a naval reserve training vessel moored in Lorain Harbor got word to Cleveland, and news of the destruction in Lorain began to leak out to the world. The poor operator had been a witness to the storm; terrible as it was, he thought it was much worse and told everyone that thousands were dead. Receiving this news, the people of Cleveland, and other towns in Ohio, galvanized into action.

The bicycle messengers told similar tales, and it is understandable how they misjudged the death toll. They left a city where the downtown was a scene of total destruction. Proud buildings lay crumbled and streetcars overturned, and bodies, half buried in debris, were everywhere.

7:30 p.m., Lorain

The longest day of the year had passed seven days earlier, but the anguished survivors of the tornado were keenly aware that daylight would be gone in several hours. There were so many injured and dead and no electric lights to help in the search.

Deaths at the State Theater were especially random.

People who congregated on Broadway looked with dazed horror at what was once a beautiful building. Now it was a pile of rubble, and in that mess were at least one hundred people. Thank God there weren't more, they told one another.

Earlier in the day, more than one thousand people, mostly students, had been watching the early matinee. They had left the theater only thirty minutes before the killer storm struck. Now the stunned survivors of the second showing were being pulled out of the ruins. If conscious, they would cry for loved ones still trapped or dead.

The rescue at the State Theater would be a long and laborious effort. Besides the people in the theater, there were also the occupants of three stories of apartments that had crashed down into the theater below. Bathtubs, furniture, iceboxes and clothes littered the debris field and had to be lifted with great care.

Slowly, the living and the dead were pulled from the site.

Sam Burns told rescuers that he had been in the theater when the tornado struck. He was watching the beginning of the movie when he heard the roof collapse. He ran into the lobby and huddled next to a billboard advertising the upcoming movie *A Lone Chance*. He decided it was an omen—his last chance. He survived almost unscathed.

Another man rushed to the theater to get his two daughters and raced out, not realizing one of the little girls he had saved was not his child. Luckily, his other daughter crawled out of the theater, not seriously hurt.

After several hours, the rescuers found the projectionist at the State Theater. James Brandos had fallen to the basement still enclosed in his projection booth and was found unharmed.

8:30 p.m., Lorain

As darkness began to fall, the residential areas slipped into the shadows, creating a scene from a macabre movie. Carrying candles and lanterns, people searched for loved ones, calling out names in the dusky, falling light. Sometimes there was a response, but mostly there was silence. There was the heartbreaking weeping of those who had lost everything. As night fell, the disembodied moans and cries of people trapped in debris floated through the eerie darkness, pleading for help.

St. Joseph's Hospital was a three-story building between Twentieth and Twenty-first Streets. Within hours, the small structure was jammed with the wounded, many critically. Without power, light was necessary, and someone came up with the idea of lining up cars outside facing the hospital and turning on their headlights. This helped a bit, as did the candles and lanterns brought in by caregivers, but it was terrible for the doctors and nurses who had to perform surgery by car light and candles.

8:45 p.m., Lorain

Harry Buttle died at the hospital from perforated lungs sustained in the collapse of the Lakeview bathhouse. His death was the third in his family.

9:00 p.m., Lorain

To add to the confusion, many of the doctors from Lorain were in Germany for a medical conference, leaving the stricken city short of medical staff. Frantic telegrams were sent out from Cleveland asking for their quick return, but everyone knew it would be several weeks before they would complete the transatlantic crossing and arrive back in town.

As more and more patients arrived, the high school began to take in the overflow, and the Red Cross and nurses and doctors from Cleveland and Elyria began to arrive to care for the victims who needed medical attention.

Sadly, as the death count began to grow, the high school was turned into a morgue. Blankets covered the bodies, and if it was known, a little note with a name was put on each corpse. As the night progressed and word got out about the morgue, hundreds of people began to arrive and silently search for loved ones. The silence was torn only with crying and wailing when a person was discovered to be dead.

Down at the site of the Crystal Restaurant, five-year-old George and his sister, Cookie LaLonde, pulled themselves out of the ruins of the building. George and his sister both had head injuries, and his sister had a spike driven into her arm. Dazed and in shock, they began to wander around Lorain looking for their mother.

The Foisy family to the east did not have to look far for father Louis. As they crawled out of the basement of what had been their home, they found his body a short distance away, lying in the street. Around him were the shattered remains of their house. The tornado had lifted Louis, along with the house, into the air and then smashed everything on the ground below.

9:00 p.m., Lorain

Catherine LaLonde was lying under an icebox in the ruins of the Crystal Restaurant. When rescuers freed her, she became conscious. Her injuries included a severely broken arm, but when told by someone that her children had left, she began to walk the destroyed streets of Lorain calling for them in the dark. No one thought to tell her that two children, not three, had left the collapsed building.

9:15 p.m.

Joseph Michalek's wife and children began praying for his safe return.

Mary Peters had stayed in the basement until she decided it was safe to come upstairs with her children. By some miracle, her house was safe, and her husband finally made it home, weeping with joy to find his family alive. His business was badly damaged, and it had taken hours to help the traumatized customers who had been inside reach their homes. Mary wanted to call her brother in Elyria to let him know she was safe, but John Peters explained that all communication was down.

The fate of their boarder was unknown. After telling Mary and the children to go into the cellar, he had disappeared. He was never seen again.

Help came from all over, but the first to respond were rescue crews from Elyria and Cleveland. Carpenters from the Carpenter's Union donated their time to help and were able to open at least one road so the injured could be brought to Elyria Memorial Hospital. To assist the first responders and the injured, the Rotary Club of Elyria sent a motorized soup kitchen with food and drinks.

One of the tragedies of the storm's aftermath was the fate of George Copas, age twenty, who found a way to drive an ambulance to Elyria. He worked tirelessly taking the injured to the hospital in the neighboring town. Finally, he and his partner stopped to get gas, and someone, no one knows who, tossed a lit match near the gas cans. George was killed instantly in the explosion, and his partner was severely burned.

9:30 p.m., Lorain

Within hours, the governor had called out the National Guard, and the destroyed city became an armed camp. Approximately 1,500 soldiers descended on Lorain. Martial law was established, and Brigadier General J.R. McQuigg was put in command of the Ohio National Guard. Police officers were ordered to stand duty all night, checking cars for any potential looters.

10:00 p.m., Lorain

As word spread about the disaster in Lorain, men from the outlying farming communities, Elyria and Cleveland began to make their way to the traumatized town to help dig out the injured and dead. They arrived after dark in a city without lights. Only their flares, flashlights and headlamps gave a glimpse of the vast destruction and despair of the inhabitants. As the workers trudged into town, they could hear the screams of the trapped and wounded in the surrounding darkness, and the veterans of the Great War (World War I) were reminded of the battlefields they had left only six years before.

Henry M. Baker, national director of the Red Cross, personally came to supervise the rescue. He was horrified at the destruction he encountered. He declared to the press that it was one of worst scenes had ever witnessed in his career:

> *Every building downtown was either completely or partially destroyed. The scene on Broadway is one that was never to be forgotten by those who viewed it. From Erie Avenue to Elyria Avenue extending north to south, there was a riot of destruction. Automobiles crammed inside stores or upside down. Even electrical and telephone poles were down with wires all on the streets.*

It could have been worse. George W. Irey, superintendent of the Edgewater station of the Ohio Public Utilities, saw the black funnel approaching and thought it prudent to shut down the electrical grid system. His quick action prevented what could have been disastrous fires after the storm.

10:30 p.m., Lorain

Margaret Richards's cries for help were finally answered, and some men began to dig in the rubble of the Van Deusen house. They unearthed C.E. Van Deusen alive but injured with a broken shoulder. His wife had suffered a broken arm and his son Richard, a broken leg. C.E.'s sister was slightly injured. In her arms was the body of little Wilbur, age three. Further digging unearthed the bodies of Grace and Ray Richards and the two little Richards children, Leonard and Lois.

Day Two: June 29, 1924

12:00 a.m., Cleveland

A Cleveland radio station broadcast at midnight for assistance from all towns on the northern shore region of Ohio. Specifically asked for were doctors, nurses, Red Cross workers, Salvation Army workers and ex-servicemen. The radio broadcast was a godsend to the stricken city cut off from the world in its time of greatest need. The downtown phone system was completely wiped out. Word was that repairmen were coming from as far as Cincinnati to help restore telephone and electrical service, but they wouldn't arrive until the next day.

1:00 a.m., Sandusky

Two hundred Ohio National Guardsmen marched into the center of the dark town and began to secure the area. It was ascertained that nine square blocks of the town had been severely damaged. Unlike in Lorain, the funnel had run through an industrial area on a Saturday when most people were at home.

Still, much of the downtown was severely damaged, and the National Guard was charged with the task of establishing order and helping with search and rescue. The Red Cross arrived to help, and local people gathered to assist. Plans were made to begin cleanup and rebuilding when dawn arrived.

2:00 a.m., Cleveland

The *City of Erie* was base in Cleveland. Its regular run was Cleveland to Erie to Buffalo and back, and it was dubbed the "Honeymoon Special" because so many newlyweds bound for Niagara Falls took the ship to Buffalo. In the early hours of June 29, its mission was far more grim. It slipped away from the docks in Cleveland carrying medical supplies and personnel. It was not publicized at the time, but the ship also carried over one hundred coffins for use by the expected dead.

3:00 a.m., Lorain

The Salvation Army arrived in Lorain at 3:00 a.m. with five hundred sandwiches and ninety gallons of coffee. Under the direction of Captain L.M. Pervier and Captain Jeffries of the Salvation Army, the relief organization brought workers assigned to distribute food and drink to the needy. A druggist from Youngstown drove all night to bring medical supplies to the city.

3:30 a.m., Lorain

The lights from the *City of Erie* were spotted in Lorain Harbor. Medical help had arrived at last. It was desperately needed. Injured people were coming to the first-aid centers and hospital by any means possible. Some came by ambulance but most by car or on foot. Others were brought by stretcher or carried by family and friends. A few people were even brought for medical attention in wheelbarrows.

6:00 a.m., Lorain

With daylight, the rescue work took on a new speed. Of immediate concern was finding the injured and then recovering the dead. But the living had to be considered, too. The Ohio National Guard took the lead by arriving with tents for the homeless, which they quickly set up. Soon, tent cities were appearing all over Lorain.

As the sun came up over the disaster area, it confirmed the worst fears of the living: yesterday's storm had not just been a nightmare, and for many people, their lives had changed forever. Loss of loved ones, destroyed homes and businesses and injuries both life threatening and minor had to be faced. Others faced financial ruin. Very few people had the type of insurance that protected them against tornado damage.

In the rubble and debris of what had once been proud homes, there still arose the faint cries for help, although the voices were now weaker and harder to locate. Rescue workers carrying picks and shovels went from spot to spot to dig out the trapped people. Others used their hands as they desperately tried to reach those buried alive.

It was the same in the shattered downtown district. The city was a mob of military and conscripted men working to clear buildings with their bare hands. It was felt that heavy equipment could further injure or kill those trapped under the bricks and concrete.

At a time when most people would be preparing for religious services and church bells would be ringing, this Sunday morning was oddly silent. The chimes in nine churches were quiet, the buildings partially or totally destroyed. Weeping parishioners, stunned from the terrible night they had spent, arrived for early services only to find shells of the buildings where they had once worshipped. It was a loss to many of the survivors who now desperately needed the solace of their faith to get through the days ahead.

Besides the damage to the churches, daylight brought the realization that many schools in the city were either destroyed or damaged. The school buildings of Charleston, Irving Junior High, Harrison, Fairhome, Longefellow and Brownell were badly damaged. Charleston was eventually considered unsalvageable and was torn down.

7:30 a.m., Lorain

It had been a sleepless night for Clara Lodwick, a Red Cross nurse. She was one of the first nurses to arrive at the scene of the disaster and was quickly appointed supervisor of nursing services for the Red Cross Northern Ohio Tornado Relief Effort. A determined and dedicated young woman with a degree in public health nursing, Clara was the perfect person to initiate the arduous first steps of bringing order to chaos.

Her superior, Harry Baker, had immediately set up offices in the Antlers Hotel on West Erie Street. Completed in 1923, the new structure was constructed under modern guidelines with steel beams and reinforced concrete. These new requirements enabled the hotel to withstand the onslaught of the storm. Consequently, it became the headquarters for all the organizations starting to pour into Lorain to give help to the city.

Clara began to organize the dozens of nurses who were arriving from Cleveland. Not only did she have to decide where these women would work, but she also had to find housing, food and transportation for them. Some nurses would be needed to man the medical stations being set up throughout the city, while others were needed in hospital units. Other nurses had to be sent out to make house calls on injured or traumatized victims. It was also necessary to coordinate the nurses with the doctors and volunteers, placing them strategically for maximum benefit.

After doing as much as she could to organize the Red Cross nursing relief effort, Clara would have put on her Red Cross cap and red cape and gone out to see what needed to be done. She would have carried her first-aid supplies in her carrier so when she came across a person in need of help, she would be ready to assist.

Rescue workers had toiled throughout the night at Lakewood Park, working by torchlight and fires built on the beach to find anyone left alive. Occasionally during the endless night, the waves would splash a broken body, most certainly dead, on the sand. Men ran up and down the beach netting the corpses and bringing them to shore before the lake reclaimed them for good.

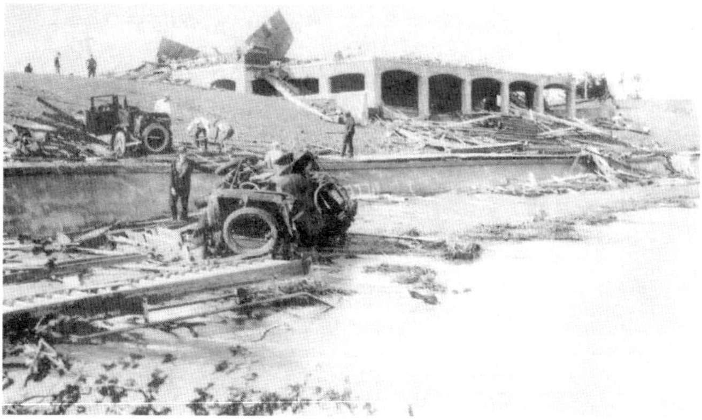

The 1924 tornado made landfall at Lakeview Park beach. The two-story bathhouse was the site of many deaths and injuries. *Courtesy of the Lorain Public Library.*

Closer to the bathhouse, there were more fires. It was a backbreaking task to lift the heavy bricks and stone slabs to find trapped bathers. Work was spurred on by the occasional low cries and moans from those buried alive. Then a hand or foot would appear, and someone would be pulled alive from the ruins. It was a macabre sight, whether the person was dead or alive. Everyone was covered with a heavy white film of dust streaked with red blood.

The *Cleveland Plain Dealer* reporter at the scene wrote about two children, Edith, age two, and her four-year-old brother, Donald, as they were pulled out of the ruins with only minor injuries. Their parents were seriously injured in the collapse of the bathhouse, and their grandmother, Eunice Beam, had been killed instantly.

By morning, the beach began to resemble a salvage yard. Volunteers combed the water's edge, dragging in pieces of cars, houses and bodies. It would take several days before Lake Erie gave up most of its dead. How many were actually swept into the lake and killed is impossible to say because there was a transient population in Lorain—people passing through, workers without families to search for them. Gawkers came in full force to watch the rescue operations on the beach.

Mary Kodelja's body came in with the waves. The coroner would later say she died from drowning.

8:30 a.m., Lorain

Besides the lethal power of a tornado's funnel to suck up everything in its path, the winds surrounding the storm are merciless. They drive anything and everything, creating projectiles that soar through the air and impale objects in their path. Unfortunately, human beings are often the recipients of the storm's flotsam.

This was the case in Lorain. The winds of the tornado had sucked up thousands of items and turned them into weapons. Flying wooden boards, embedded with nails, impaled many people. Now, seventeen hours after the tornado struck the city, doctors and nurses at makeshift first-aid centers and hospitals toiled to set broken bones, sew up flesh torn from muscle and remove objects that the violent wind had driven into helpless bodies.

As wounded citizens crawled out of the rubble, the numbers who staggered to the medical tents or were brought there by others was confounding. Doctors worked to remove metal poles driven into legs and torsos, wooden sticks imbedded in cracked skulls. Many people came for help with terrible cuts caused by the flying glass. One example of these types of injuries was the case of two men who were caught on a street corner when the wind rose, heralding the tornado. One was uninjured; the other had a small metal pole driven into his pelvis with the force of hundred-mile-per-hour winds.

9:00 a.m., Lorain

George Hoffman led one thousand guardsmen to protect the city. His presence was greeted with relief. After the initial shock of the tragedy wore

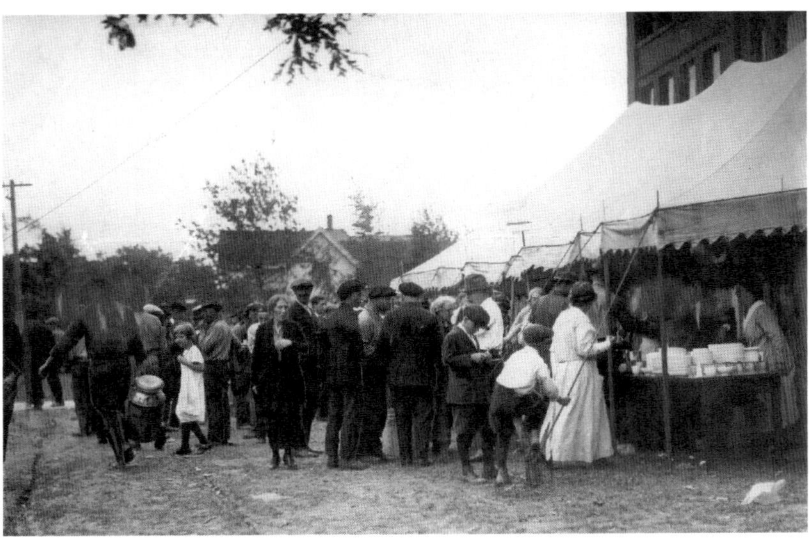

Those made homeless by the tornado receive aid at a soup kitchen. *The Cleveland Press Collection, Michael Schwartz Library, Cleveland State University.*

off, criminals from other cities tried to descend on Lorain to loot. The order was to shoot looters on sight, and reportedly, that order was carried out on several occasions. A 6:00 p.m. curfew was established and would be strictly enforced, and people were advised to stay home, if they had one, or seek shelter with family and friends.

The Red Cross began to set up tent cities, hoping to bring some order to the huge numbers of homeless people wandering around the town. Aid was starting to trickle in, faster by the hour, and the Red Cross began to sort out and arrange a system of distribution.

As more and more people were being rescued from collapsed buildings or becoming aware that they needed medical help, the first-aid centers and hospital were flooded with patients. Along with the injured came many others seeking relatives and friends. It was quickly determined that more makeshift hospitals were needed—and, unfortunately, more morgues. It was decided that South High School would become the main morgue.

10:00 a.m., Lorain

Catherine LaLonde was reunited with her two children, and despite their critical injuries, they returned to the heap of bricks, steel beams and tiles that once had been their home and the site of the Crystal Restaurant. Along with several men, they began to paw through rubble in search of Dorothy. Some people came with shovels and began to help. Mrs. Barnes, Catherine's friend, was pulled out, injured but not dead. Within hours, the body of Mary Campbell, the young waitress, was discovered, followed by the body of Edward Wittenbach, but still nothing was found of twelve-year-old Dorothy.

A little ways down the street, there was the same heartbreaking search for a loved one. Mr. Mills returned home from his fishing trip to find a scene of devastation at the business he and his wife had built. The feed store had been demolished, and there was no sign of his wife. Men arrived with a backhoe and began to dig through the rubble, moving buckets of debris. Occasionally, they would stop to listen. Hoping against hope, Mr. Mills and his teenage son, Leland, called out to Gertrude Mills, but there was no response.

11:00 a.m., Lorain

The largest number of rescue workers was at the State Theater. The four-story building was now just a heap of rubble, but everyone knew that at least one hundred people might be buried in that debris, and many of them were teenagers and children.

Working with lanterns and car lights, the rescuers had spent the previous night pulling injured people out of the remains of the stricken theater. Now, hours later, the work had increased rather than slowed down. As in other spots, it was deemed too dangerous to bring in heavy equipment to lift up the huge blocks of concrete, bricks and steel beams. As a result, the rescue effort was a nonstop human endeavor—digging, lifting and carrying rubble away so rescuers could reach the basement. It was felt that many of the people in the theater had plunged to the lowest point in the building.

This assumption was correct.

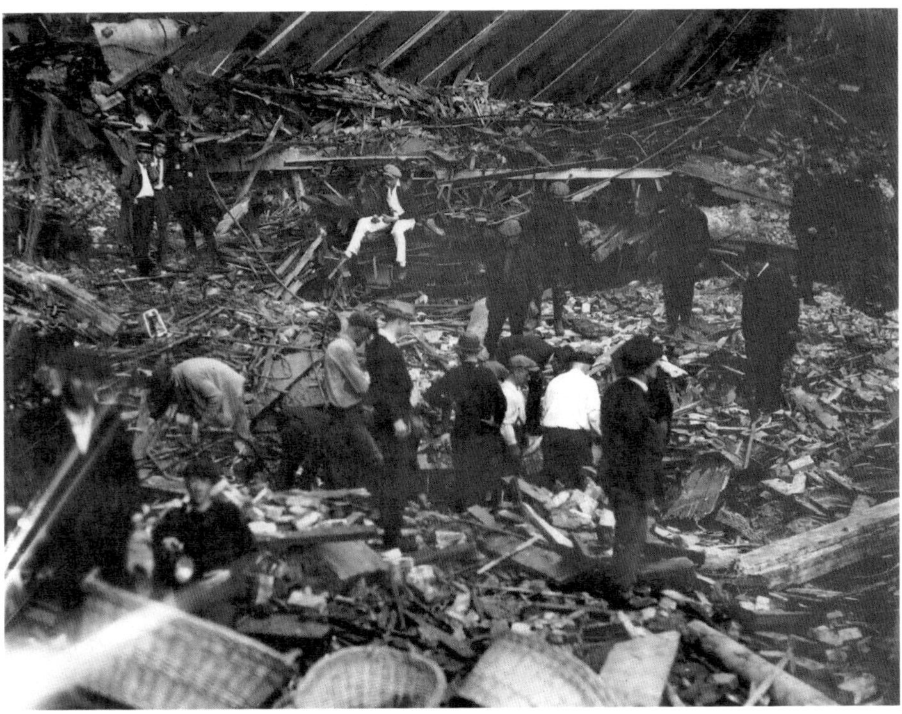

Work crews struggle to find survivors in the wreckage of the State Theater. *The Cleveland Press Collection, Michael Schwartz Library, Cleveland State University.*

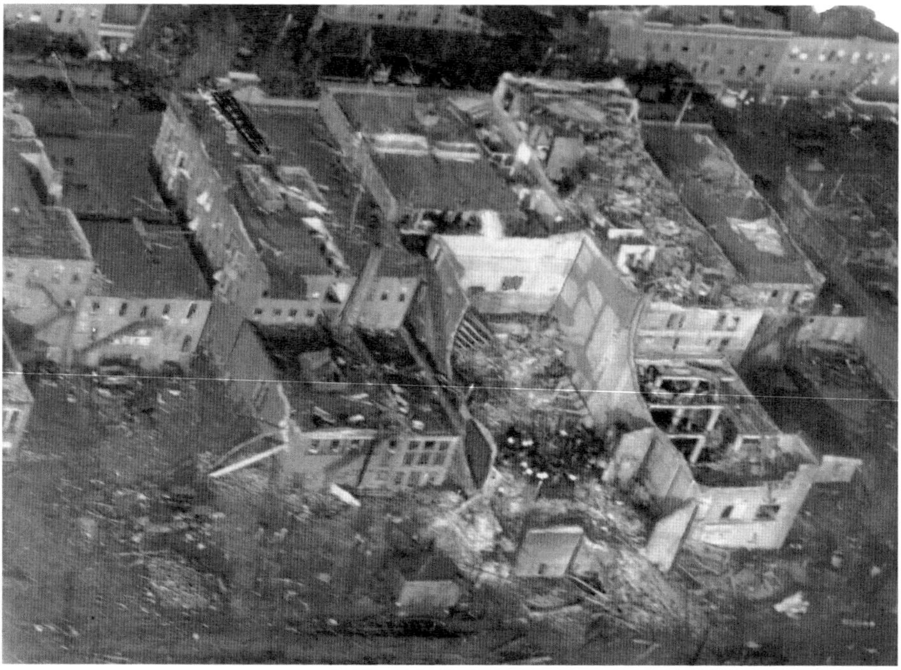

Aerial view of the State Theater, which had been a four-story building. Approximately 250 people were in the theater when the upper stories collapsed onto the first floor. *The Cleveland Press Collection, Michael Schwartz Library, Cleveland State University.*

12:30 p.m., Lorain

The bodies of Catherine and Joseph Blinzely were pulled from the bathhouse and Lakeview Park beach. Work was progressing slowly. The top floor of the bathhouse had been totally demolished, and many of the severely injured were unearthed in this area. The basement area had many injured, too, so every piece of concrete—every beam, every brick—had to be carefully removed so as not to further injure someone lying below.

The work continued without a break, revealing more bodies and even more injured. It was hot work, but no one was eager to cool off in the waters of the lake.

1:00 p.m., Lorain

The extent of the injured was just being realized. The steamer *City of Erie* had offloaded its grim cargo and was now ready to return to Cleveland, so it was decided to evacuate the most seriously injured to Cleveland hospitals as quickly as possible. It was hoped that the steamer would make good time back to Cleveland. This turned out to be impossible. An unforeseen problem was that the tornado had whipped up the water, not only on the lake, but also on the Black River, and the steamship was unable to safely cast off its moorings to depart.

This was a terrible delay for the patients, many of whom were grievously injured, lying on stretchers throughout the packed boat. The moans of suffering were terrible to hear. Two sisters, Olga and Florence Nickley, were very badly injured, and it was hoped they could be saved in the Cleveland hospital. Olga, age twelve, had a fractured leg and spine. Her six-year-old sister, Florence, had even worse internal injuries. Nearby was Gertrude Fisk, whose house had imploded around her, fracturing her skull.

Although only the wounded were supposed to be on board, along with accompanying medical personnel, there were several stowaways who refused to leave their injured friends and family members. One teenager named Joe Rego refused to abandon his seriously injured buddy, John Sepos, age fourteen, and was finally allowed to stay on board. The local newspapers recounted his adventures:

> *I was sitting in Mrs. Julia Szabo's house...the wind broke in all the windows, the house lifted up and the floor fell in...I was being thrown through the air. I landed two blocks away. But that ain't nothing. Johnny had the whole house lying on his head and arm, when they dragged him out.*

Joe went to Cleveland with his friend and stayed at the hospital with John until he recovered.

2:30 p.m., Lorain

Mrs. Michalek and her five children prayed that Joseph Michalek would return home. It was difficult to find out any news in the devastated city. They went to the Lorain High School morgue, but his body was not there. This raised their hopes, and they began to search for him, but to no avail.

Mrs. Michalek and her children continued to search.

2:40 p.m., Lorain

The Amish farmers from central Ohio arrived, driving into town in their horse-drawn buggies. They were expert roofers, and they came to offer help fixing many damaged buildings. Their arrival was met with relief. The latest count declared that seven thousand people were homeless from the tornado. More than five hundred homes were destroyed, and another one

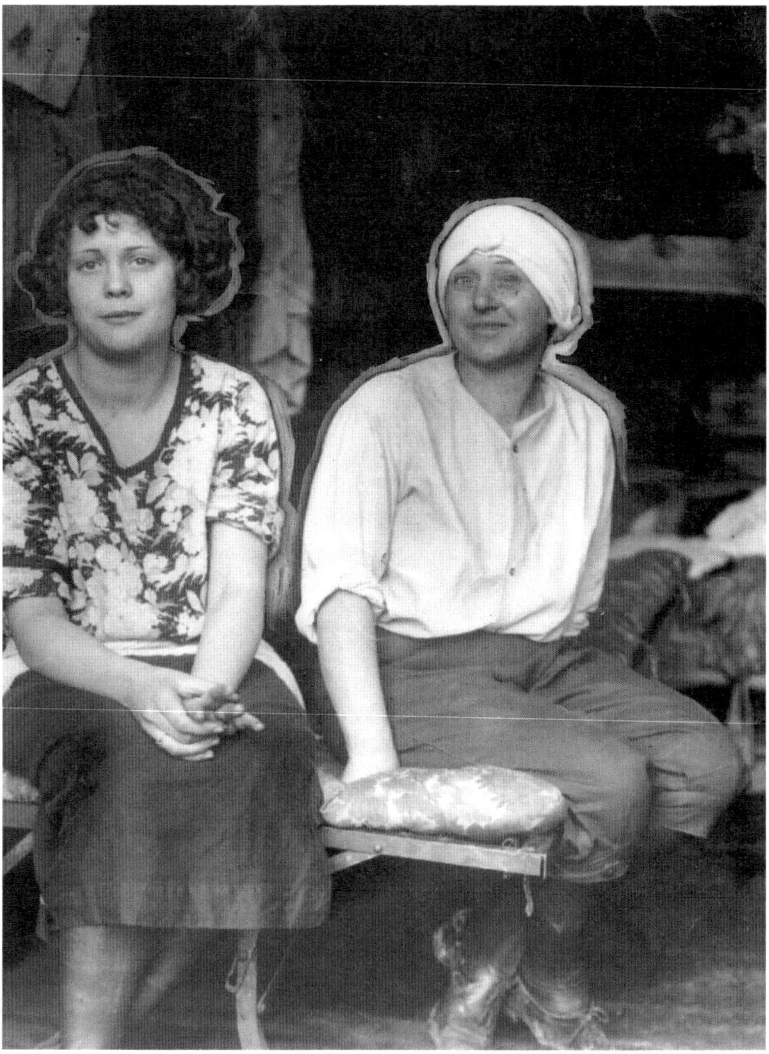

Tornado victims seek shelter. *The Cleveland Press Collection, Michael Schwartz Library, Cleveland State University.*

thousand were damaged, many badly. What this meant was that in a city of approximately forty thousand people, almost one-quarter of the population no longer had a place to live.

3:00 p.m., Lorain

Finally, after several dangerous attempts, the *City of Erie* cast off for Cleveland, loaded down with injured patients. Another piece of good news was that 150 linesmen from all over northern Ohio were desperately trying to restore power to the most needy areas.

4:00 p.m., Lorain

Alerted by telegraph, news of the catastrophe was coursing through the nation. Reporters and photographers were arriving by the minute to record the disaster. By late afternoon, anxious relatives from neighboring towns trudged into Lorain, often having walked for miles. Tragically, many made it to their destination only to find nothing but splintered wood where homes once stood. Unable to find those they sought, they were advised to go to the hospitals and the morgues.

Traveling around the city was very difficult. In the residential districts, tree branches and rubble from houses blocked the streets. Downtown, it was a confusion of overturned trolley cars, smashed automobiles and fallen buildings. The B&O ore bridge that spanned the Black River was twisted into a heap of metal, and the unlucky Nickel Plate drawbridge was out of commission, too.

To make matters worse, South Lorain, which did not experience the windstorm damage, was now suffering from floodwaters brought in by the tornado. In some places, the water was three to four feet deep, and almost all basements were flooded.

6:00 p.m., Lorain

The National Guard was determined that the 6:00 p.m. curfew would be strictly enforced. Guardsman moved systematically through the streets ordering people to return to their homes or places of shelter. Often this was met with resistance by the still dazed and shocked citizens who had lost loved ones or were still searching as they wandered the streets.

The only people allowed to ignore the curfew were the rescue workers who labored to uncover victims. Armed guards worked alongside them to make sure looting did not occur by someone pretending to be a rescue worker.

11:00 p.m., Lorain

The LaLonde family, along with rescuers, worked into the night to find Dorothy. Their search ended just before midnight, when Dorothy's body was discovered. She was in the basement of the restaurant, wedged between two ovens, one from her family's apartment and one from the restaurant. Her father was still out on the lake and unable to help his grieving family. No commercial vessels were allowed to dock in Lorain and had to go to other ports, such as Toledo, Buffalo or Erie.

As they covered the broken body of the twelve-year-old girl, there was flickering light down the street. Mr. Mills and his crew were still searching for Gertrude Mills.

Day Three: June 30, 1924

9:00 a.m., Lorain

It was finally decided that excavating at the State Theater was going too slowly, and dangerous as it was, a steam shovel would have to be brought to the site to help in the search for survivors.

This decision was met with relief by the large crew, consisting mainly of National Guardsmen, volunteers and conscripted laborers (those who had violated martial law) and gawkers. This last group was a desperate attempt by the military to get more manpower. Any able-bodied man who was seen "gawking" around town was given a shovel and told to get to work. Saying "no" was not an option.

9:30 a.m., Cleveland

Charles Fisk was informed that his wife, Gertrude, had died from the fractured skull sustained in the destruction of their home.

10:00 a.m., Lorain

Short-wave radio, intrepid reporters and military briefings sent out updates of the tragedy in Lorain. The Pennsylvania Railroad Company had employees make their own reports. On June 30, 1924, a memorandum advised the main staff in Pittsburg as follows about the situation in Lorain, Ohio:

> *The city is under martial law and they are trying to keep everybody off the streets except rescue workers. They had no lights last night and used automobile lights for lighting purposes…Starting today to remove debris, digging the State Theater first trying to remove the bodies. The death list now stands at 59, but on account of the bad condition no accurate estimate can be made of the property damage…It is thought that quite a few bodies will be found in the houses wrecked. All of the available telegraph line is badly congested with messages of friends and relatives trying to ascertain information…In addition to the National Guardsmen there are one hundred twenty policemen from Cleveland...Superintendent Dorsey of the LA & S Railroad was not permitted to go to his office yesterday on account of martial law prohibiting person from entering buildings.*

The report continued:

> *At four thirty p.m. June 28th, a cyclone accompanied by heavy rain struck this town, destroying the eastern part of town. The situation in Sandusky, Ohio is as follows…Six known dead and one hundred reported hurt. Property loss estimated at $2,000,000.00…The city was without water and lights as of last night.*

11:00 a.m., a Farm East of Cleveland

Not only were lives lost, but also pets, livestock, furniture and personal items. A great deal of the city had been blown into the lake, but some items were blown as far away as sixty miles. Esther Smallwood, in her 2001 remembrance of the tornado, recalled that her family farm east of Cleveland was littered with papers, books and photographs from Lorain. Only nine years old at the time, she remembered going out to the pasture and picking up photographs, books and other items the tornado had seized in Lorain and then capriciously dumped on her family farm.

12:00 p.m., Lorain

The situation with the seven thousand homeless was critical. Some people sought shelter with friends and relatives. Others moved to neighboring towns. But most people without homes moved to the tent cities that were being set up in Lorain and surrounding towns.

Others stubbornly refused to abandon their damaged homes. On June 30, a photographer took a photograph of a woman sitting in her living room writing at her desk. This picture would run on July 1. The front walls of the house had been destroyed, but the rest of the house, resembling a dollhouse, stood upright.

The crew laboring at the State Theater made a grim discovery. The steam shovel had unearthed enough rubble to reveal four bodies wedged under fallen beams. They were in a precarious spot, so the decision was made not to try to remove them at this time because the instability of the ruins could endanger anyone below. Fighting back their horror and sadness, the men went back to work.

1:00 p.m., Lorain

Red Cross nurse Clara Lodwick's organizational skills were put to good use. The city of Lorain was divided into five districts for home visiting nurses. It was decided that the entire visiting nurse program would be under the supervision of the American Red Cross, and each nurse would be paid $150 a month, plus gasoline and oil expenses. Nurse Lodwick even took the time to arrange for one gas station to provide all the gas and oil for the Red Cross.

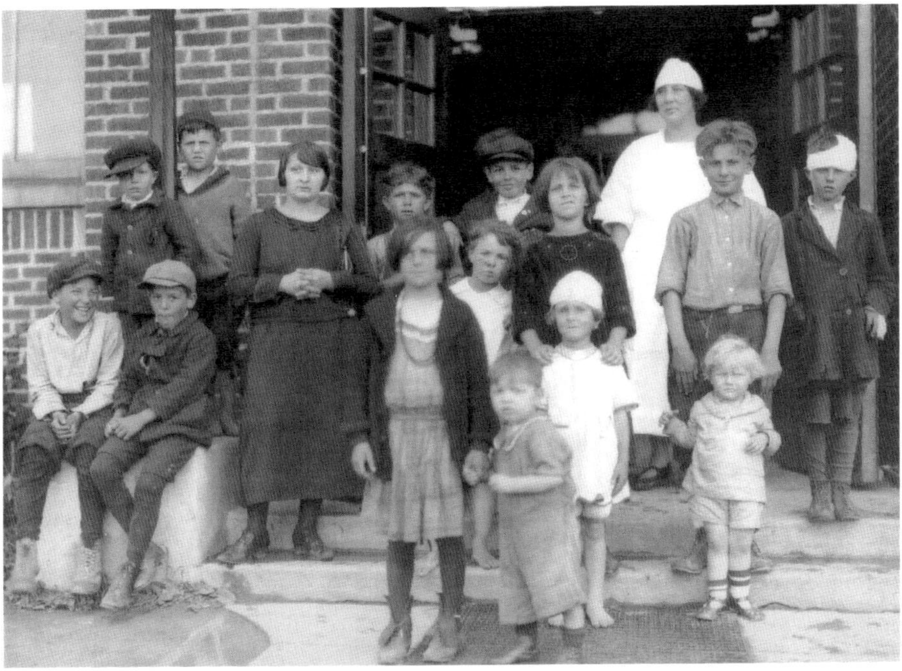

Above: Children pose in front of a hospital after the storm. *The Cleveland Press Collection, Michael Schwartz Library, Cleveland State University.*

Right: Injured children pose in front of a hospital. *The Cleveland Press Collection, Michael Schwartz Library, Cleveland State University.*

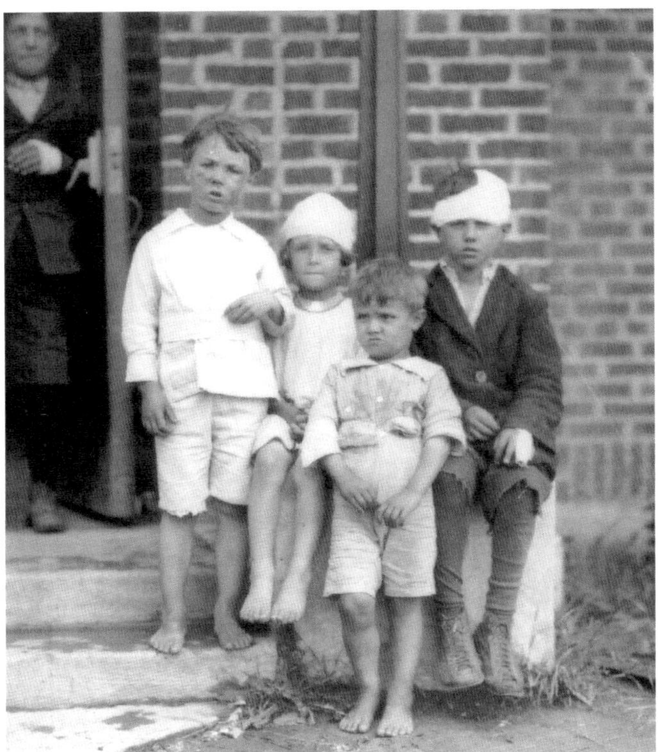

1:30 p.m., Lorain

In Lorain, an unsavory element was drifting into town from Cleveland and Chicago, so the National Guard became even stricter with thieves. A corral was established on the corner of Twelfth Street and Broadway to house anyone breaking the military regulations. Violators were herded into the corral until authorities could decide what to do with them. Putting them in jail was out of the question, for it was standing room only in the area reserved for inmates. Some prisoners who had committed minor crimes were simply released to make room for more serious cases.

The mayor drafted resolutions that would go into effect on July 2, 1924. Only people who had official business or owned property in the damaged areas of the city were allowed to enter during the day. Between 8:00 p.m. and 5:00 a.m., only military authorities were allowed to enter this area. All deaths and missing persons were to be reported to the Military Pass Office. People were urged to be calm and patient. In essence, military law prevailed.

In another attempt to bring order to chaos, the police set up a Bureau of Identification and posted the following notice in all pertinent newspapers and in signs around the town:

> *Bureau of Identification has been established at Lorain to handle all bodies and inquiries relative to missing persons. Anyone having information or inquiries concerning missing persons are requested to report them at the Bureau office located in Police Chief Walker's office, Police Station, Erie Street, Lorain.*

A man by the name of Roy Richards and his father rushed to Lorain when they received word that Harry Richards had died in the tornado. They received permission to search for Harry's body, but just as they were leaving the Military Pass Office, in walked Harry. It turned out that the person who had told them Harry was dead had confused their relative with Ray Richards of Columbus, who died in the collapse of the Van Deusen home.

4:00 p.m., Lorain

State Theater rescue workers unearthed the body of a woman in her thirties and were able to safely dislodge the beams around her. The dead woman was lifted out of the rubble and sent to the makeshift morgue. It was speculated that she lived in one of the apartments above the theater and had died when the upper floors collapsed under the weight of the Wickham Building roof.

Shortly after discovering the dead woman, the rescue workers reached the basement of the State Theater building. It was still slow going, with each piece of rubble lifted out by hand. Forty-eight hours after the storm, three little girls were found in the wreckage. Margaret Powers, five, was not conscious, and her right hip and leg were broken, along with her left arm. Nearby lay Anna and Helen Hanyak. The sisters were playing quietly together, though both had suffered internal injuries. Next to them was the body of Audrey Pressick, age nine.

The men who lifted the little girls out of the basement were grimly aware that there were still more people in there.

8:30 p.m., Lorain

Several blocks away, rescuers toiled day and night to find the remains of Gertrude Mills. Twenty-five truckloads of debris were hauled away before they reached the basement of the Mills Feed Store. The crushed and unrecognizable body of Gertrude Mills was discovered under tons of feedbags.

Astoundingly, a crate with newborn chickens, eight in all, was found nearby. All the chicks were fine.

Day Four: July 1, 1924

The first day of July, the funerals began.

10:00 a.m., Sandusky

It must be remembered that Sandusky was the initial town to feel the deadly impact of the tornado. In the end, it was determined that seven people lost their lives in the city.

On July 1, Sandusky held a public funeral for five of the victims: R.F. McKee, William Hampton, Howard Vanbiarcumb, Jacob Shaefer and Minetta Margard. The solemn procession wove through town to take the bodies to the graveyard. The citizens of Sandusky turned out in large numbers to honor the dead.

It was announced that Howard Wobser would be buried privately on July 2. The seventh victim, John Hinton, was from Kentucky, and as of July 1, no one had been able to reach his family.

11:00 a.m., Lorain

Twenty-four funerals were planned for this day alone.

Most people at this time were "waked" at home. Because many of the dead had lost their own homes, friends and relatives—sometimes even strangers—offered their homes for the services. Many people went from house to house to pay last visits to people they knew. It was calculated that

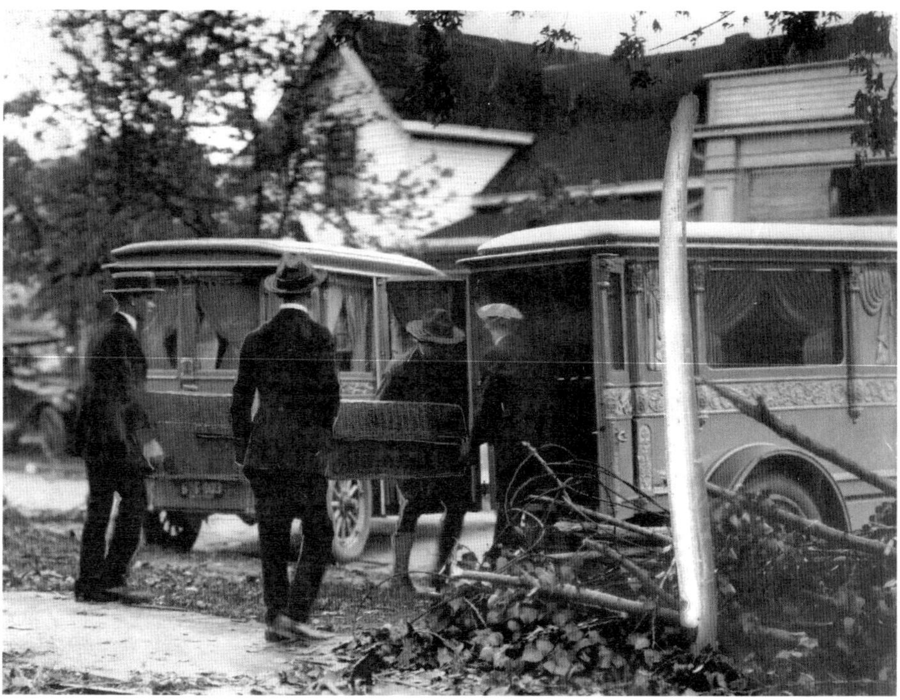

A victim of the tornado is being placed in a hearse. Wakes were held at home. *The Cleveland Press Collection, Michael Schwartz Library, Cleveland State University.*

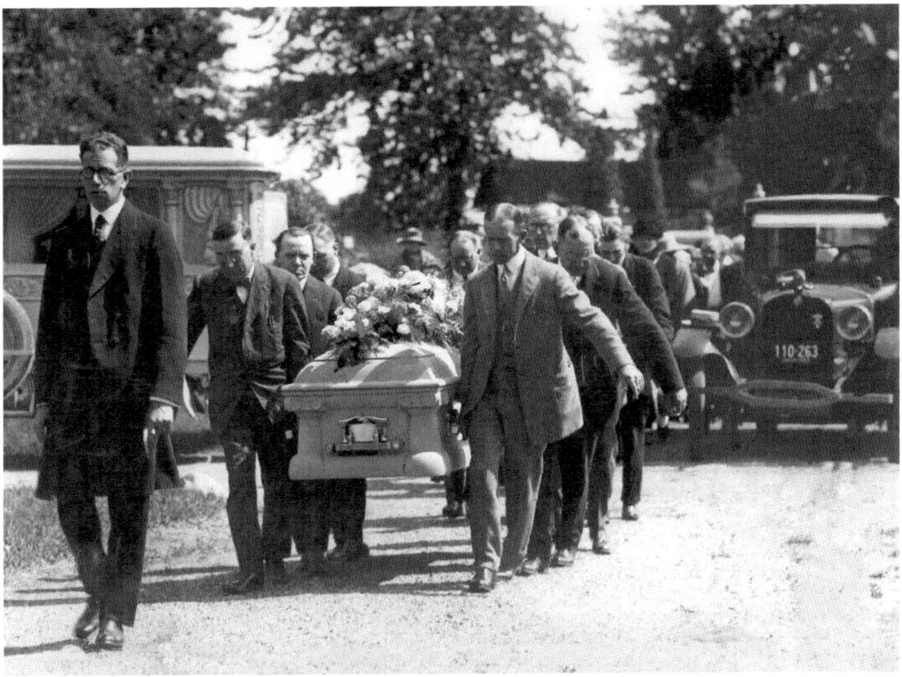

Funeral for a victim of the storm. *The Cleveland Press Collection, Michael Schwartz Library, Cleveland State University.*

seventy-two people were killed in Lorain and over one thousand injured severely enough that they needed medical care. This was a serious blow to the close-knit citizens of Lorain.

With at least seventy-two funerals in the coming week, the city council limited the numbers of mourners going to the cemetery to immediate family. It was felt that with so many deaths and so many funerals that large parties of mourners would further hurt the town's morale.

One of the funerals was for Gertrude Mills.

12:00 p.m., Lorain

As the dead were being buried, the search for more victims continued.

At the State Theater, the grim work went on. At first, the rescuers toiled by hand to free any survivors, but the wreckage was so great and so deep that the steam-powered backhoe now lifted most of the debris. To make matters worse, on Monday, July 1, heavy rain began to fall, forcing the rescue teams to call off the search until the next day. Buried by rubble and collapsed furniture from above, it would take several days to free anyone else who was trapped.

In all, fifteen people, most of them teenagers and children, died in the collapse of the State Theater—the largest number of people to die in an Ohio theater to this day. Survivors commented that the last song they heard was Mary Hirsch playing "Sacrifice" on the piano in the orchestra pit.

The body of twelve-year-old Bessie Widzer, whose parents had escaped Czarist-occupied Latvia and whose sister died in the Spanish flu epidemic, was finally discovered in the basement of the State Theater under mountains of debris covered by steel beams. Close by were the bodies of several other teenagers. Her parents decided to bury her at the Salem Jewish Cemetery.

Three days after the storm, rescue workers finally lifted the broken smokestack at the American Shipbuilding Plant. Underneath was the body of Joseph Michalek. It had been hidden from view by the smashed smokestack that landed on him when the funnel sucked him out of the building. His body was taken to a small morgue set up nearby because the high school morgue was now filled to capacity.

A man was sent to tell his family of the grim discovery.

His wife would have to raise their five children alone.

In nearby Elyria Memorial Hospital, C.E. Van Duesen was recovering from his injuries, along with his son, Richard, who had suffered a broken leg. His wife and sister were recovering at the home of a friend as they made arrangements for the funeral of little Wilbur. The other four who died in the house would be buried in Columbus.

On a positive note, power was restored to St. Joseph's Hospital on July 1, greatly aiding the doctors and nurses in their care of the patients. Now they could work under electric lights rather than hand-held lanterns and car lights. Also on July 1, it was announced that all roads leading to Lorain were now open, except for Lake Road, which was still clogged with trees and debris.

Adding to the confusion was all the devastation at the waterfront. The harbor was still blocked with damaged boats and timber, and the Black River's current continued too strong for any real navigation. The three main bridges, the E Street and the Nickel Plate, were both still out of commission, as was the B&O Railroad bridge. It was estimated that many of the boats in harbor would have to wait another week before offloading or departing the city.

Slowly, the focus was turning from the dead and injured to anxiety about the well-being of the living. Fear of contagious illness was increasing, so the Health Department began to circulate warnings and precautions. Smallpox was greatly feared, as were typhoid and diphtheria. Another worry was contaminated water.

The state health department set up precautions to prevent the spread of disease. In an era before antibiotics, minor infections could easily become gangrenous, so caution was urged to take care of all wounds immediately. Another, more gruesome side of the storm not often mentioned were all the dead animals and birds whose bodies began to rot in the summer heat. Provisions were made to pick up carcasses left near curbs.

The National Guard supervised repairs and search and rescue efforts. A proclamation was issued from the head of the National Guard that all looters were to be shot on sight. The curfew was changed to last from 8:00 p.m. to 5:00 a.m. Where workers labored to uncover debris, passes were assigned so that looters and thieves could be contained.

By July 1, some power had been restored to two dairies, the undertakers' facilities, city hall and the city jail.

3:00 p.m., Cleveland

Florence Nickley, age six, succumbed to her injuries and died at a Cleveland hospital. Her sister, Olga, remained in critical condition but was expected to live.

4:00 p.m., Sandusky

By July 1, it was decided to remove the majority of the National Guard in Sandusky, but the city remained under military control. The mayor asked that no one set off fireworks on the Fourth of July because of the grieving in the city and because the fire department didn't want to handle a major fire if sparks went astray.

This same restriction applied to Lorain. Thousands of people were now living with relatives or camping out in the tent cities set up by the Red Cross. Cooking and lighting was carefully monitored so fires would not start.

By July 2, 1924, streetcar service was restored to Elyria and Cleveland on a limited basis. Electricity was partially restored, and the Lorain Telephone Company announced that twenty miles of underground cable would arrive by Thursday, July 4. The telephone company had over fifty men and seven trucks engaged in cleanup work and hoped to restore service as quickly as possible.

Donations poured into the cities of Lorain and Sandusky from all over the country. The greatest number came from fellow Ohioans, as did the actual manual help. Even attempts to raise funds were turning a little lighter hearted.

Benefit dances were held to help the survivors. One at O'Loughlin's on the corner of Detroit Avenue and West Sixty-fifth Street would be held on Friday, July 25, to ease the "Suffering of Lorain Ohio. Admission—Give what you can."

Slowly, as Sandusky and Lorain buried their dead, the process of healing was underway.

Part III

CONCLUSION

The June 28, 1924 Lorain/Sandusky tornado holds the record for being the deadliest single tornado outbreak in Ohio. It also holds the record for being the fourth deadliest in the northern United States.

The death toll was set at seventy-two for Lorain, seven for Sandusky and three for the outlying farms. The Lorain total of seventy-two dead includes the eight who died in the bathhouse and the fifteen who died at the State Theater.

Not included in the total are those who died from shock sustained from the tornado. One Cleveland woman viewed the scene of the disaster in downtown Lorain and was stricken with horror. She died a week later of a heart attack. It can be assumed that there were many other people whose lives were shortened by their losses.

In the end, it was established that thirty-five blocks of the city of Lorain were directly affected by the tornado. Two hundred businesses in the downtown area were destroyed, and the rest were damaged. Five hundred houses were destroyed and another one thousand damaged, leaving more than seven thousand people in need of some type of shelter, either long or short term. The tent cities set up by Red Cross were in use for over two months.

Two hundred cars were also smashed to pieces or lying at the bottom of the lake. The debris field was so vast, and the number of cars wrecked so great, that the final number of cars actually destroyed in the storm was just an educated guess.

One piece of good news was the return of the Lorain doctors who had gone to Europe for the medical conference. It took several weeks to get back, but their patients, both old and new, were very glad to see them. The populace still desperately needed medical care. Many people sustained injuries that would take months to heal.

Red Cross nurse Clara Lodwick continued her work as long as a Red Cross nursing presence was required. Many years later, her descendants would donate all her papers and news clips to the City of Lorain Public Library. This record of information is invaluable for historians researching the 1924 tornado.

At American Shipbuilding, almost all of the building had been destroyed or sustained some kind of damage. Nonetheless, workers went back almost immediately, rebuilding, cleaning up and continuing work on different projects.

One of the most important projects was repairing the damage done to the *Henry Ford II*, commissioned by Ford Motor Company. With amazing speed, workers repaired the damage the tornado did to the ship. On August 14, 1924, just three weeks after the storm, *Henry Ford II* went out for sea trials and its first maiden voyage. It passed all tests successfully.

Henry Ford II carried freight on the Great Lakes for the Ford Motor Company for sixty-four years. In 1989, the name was changed to *Samuel Mather*, and it continued to sail until 1994, when it was sold for scrap metal.

The figures we have given for the casualties of the storm are all estimates. The numbers of losses, human or man-made, are debatable. Because of the propensity of the twister to toss objects into the lake, some people may have died and not been counted, and the confusion about the lost number of cars is the same.

But even if the number of casualties is uncertain, there is no question that the tornado of June 28, 1924, was a horrifying event. Some survivors carried painful mental and physical scars for life. For others who lived through it, the memories of what happened were terrible to recall.

As the city of Lorain began to settle down into some semblance of normalcy, there arose the big question of what to do with all the debris from the storm. It was finally decided to haul it all to the mouth of the Black River to get it out of the way. Work crews labored for months to remove the rubble so reconstruction could begin. The amount of rebuilding necessary to make Lorain whole once again was staggering.

But time passes.

The Van Deusen family repaired their home and stayed in Lorain. C.W. Van Deusen continued his law practice, and his wife was active in the community until her death in her eighties. Their two surviving children, Richard and Jean, lived long lives, married and had children of their own. Some of these children still live in the Cleveland metro area. Richard Van Deusen and his wife, Pauline, contributed greatly to today's knowledge of the tornado of 1924 by describing their own experiences on that fatal day.

As for Margaret Richards, she was taken back to Columbus by her Richards relatives. It can be assumed that she was raised in that area, though little is know about her further life.

Joseph and Catherine Blinzley were buried in Calvary Cemetery in Lorain. They were survived by two daughters and one son. The bathhouse they had lovingly managed was rebuilt and then rebuilt again.

George Lalonde and his sisters stayed in the Lorain area and contributed to the history of the town with their family experiences. Their father died in

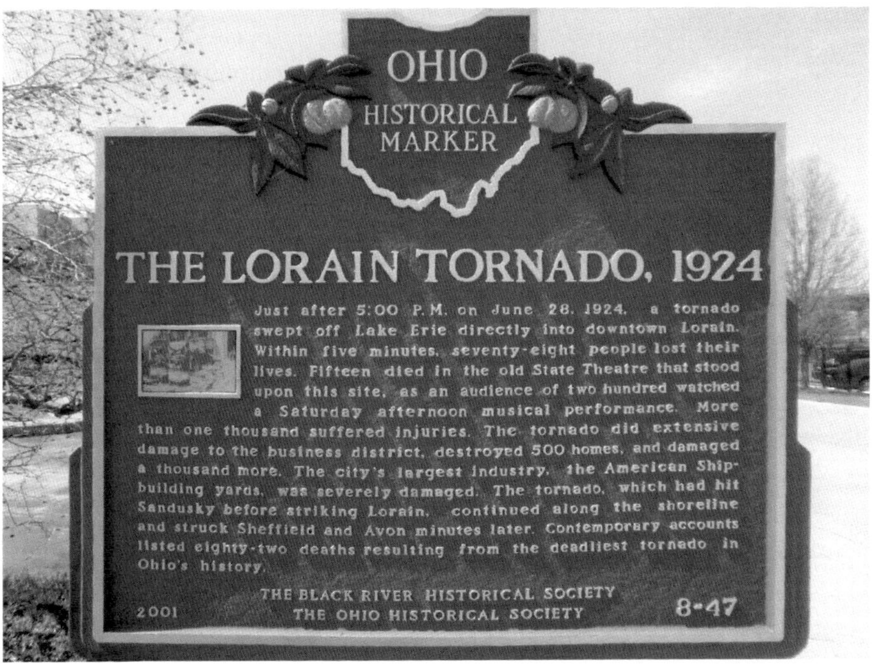

Ohio Memorial Marker at the site of the State Theater, the scene of fifteen deaths in the 1924 tornado. *Courtesy of Robert T. Smith, Elyria, Ohio.*

1944, and their mother, Catherine, lived into the 1960s. She was survived by three children and four grandchildren. Catherine LaLonde is buried next to her husband and daughter, Dorothy, in Calvary Cemetery in Lorain.

Joseph Mihalek's wife managed to keep her family together and raised her children in Lorain. One of her daughters, Charlotte, bore witness to the family's trials during the 1924 tornado. Charlotte's daughter, Carolyn Sipkovsky, and her husband live in Lorain today. They have both been active in Lorain historical societies. Carolyn was instrumental in the erection of the State Theater Memorial Marker that exists today.

The Buttle family of Brownell Avenue was one of the most hard hit in Lorain. Two siblings, Ellen Meredith and Harry Buttle, were killed, along with Harry's son, William. The parents, William and Ellen, never recovered from losing two children, a grandchild and their home, which was destroyed in the storm. They both died in 1926.

On a more positive note, the remaining two siblings lived far into the century and had full lives. George, who had sustained serious injury in the tornado, died in 1955. His brother Richard played semipro baseball as an adult and later worked at the U.S. Steel plant until his retirement. He died in 1990 at the age of ninety-nine.

The Peters family left Lorain shortly after the tornado and resettled in Athens, Greece. Mary lived into the 1970s. Their daughter Lucille married a Greek officer at the start of World War II. When he was assigned to a northern outpost of the country, she accompanied him even though she was pregnant. Lucille died in childbirth during World War II. Lucille's two brothers returned to the United States as adults and settled in Chicago. Gus Peters went on to be Cook County coroner in Chicago.

Gertrude Mills's husband later remarried and died in 1968, two years after his son, Leland, died. Some members of the large Foisy family stayed on in Lorain and contributed to the growth of the city.

Mary Kodelja's mother died as Mary Zgonc, the last name of her

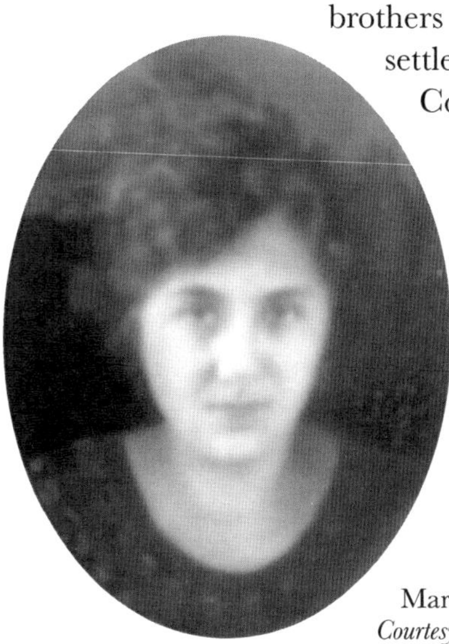

Mary Koledeja's photograph enclosed in her tombstone. *Courtesy of Robert T. Smith, Elyria, Ohio.*

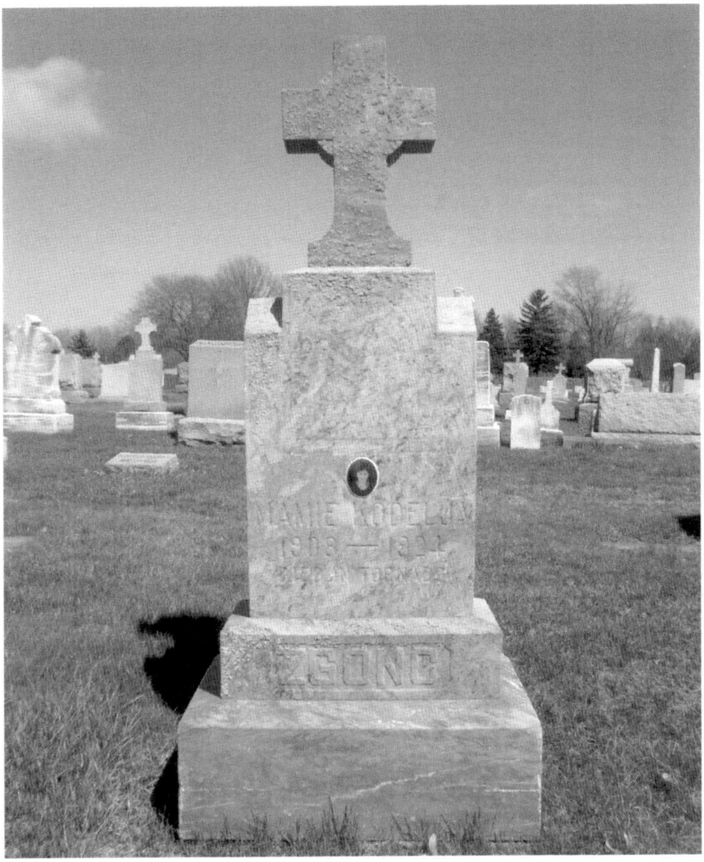

Mary Koledeja's tombstone. Mary died at Lakeview Park, one of the first victims of the tornado. *Courtesy of Robert T. Smith, Elyria, Ohio.*

second husband. She is buried next to her daughter, Mary, in Calvary Cemetery in Lorain.

The bathhouse at Lakewood Park has been reconstructed twice since 1924, and each construction contains the only standing part of the old bathhouse: a marble arch that did not fall in the tornado of 1924.

Today, Lorain Metro owns the entire park. The last major renovation was in 2007, and a new bathhouse, built on the model of the one destroyed in 1924, was constructed. It has changing rooms, a restaurant and showers. It is a popular site to visit, with a lovely café on the top deck and beautiful views of Lake Erie. Diners eating on the balcony looking over the beach can watch sunbathers and swimmers.

Memory Gardens is nearby, heady with the scent of roses in June. Besides a lovely fountain, the park has beautiful trees—all planted after 1924—which offer shade to people who want to take in the view. The park draws thousands of visitors each year.

It is a fine tribute to Mayor Leonard Moore, who, almost one hundred years ago, had the vision to see what this area could become. A three-and-a-half-ton sandstone monument with a plaque commemorating Leonard Moore can be seen today in the park. The plaque reads:

> *Memorial to Leonard M. Moore, during whose term as Mayor of Lorain, 1916–1917, this property was purchased for public park purposes. Dedicated by the youth of Lorain, Sept. 8, 1929.*

A large boulder in the park commemorates General Quincy A. Gillmore, who was born on the farm that is now the park. Another plaque is in honor of Frances E. Willard, founder of the national Woman's Christian Temperance Union.

Lorain began to rebuild, and by 1932, Lakeview Park beach was back in business sporting a new Memory Rose Garden dedicated on Memorial Day, May 30, 1932. Seventeen community organizations worked to bring the garden to bloom, and it was constructed as a wheel with eight spokes. The Rose Garden is still magnificent today and a delight when all the roses

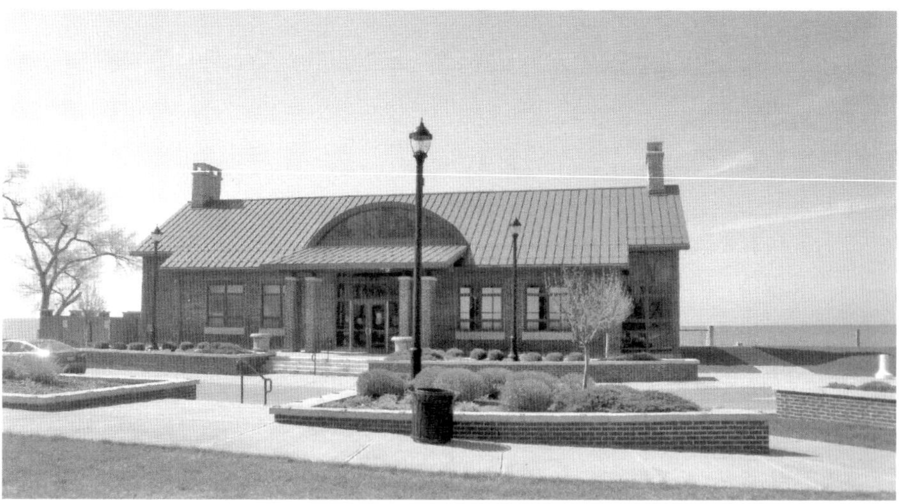

The Lakeview bathhouse today. It is owned by Lorain Metro. A restaurant is on the second floor. *Courtesy of Robert T. Smith, Elyria, Ohio.*

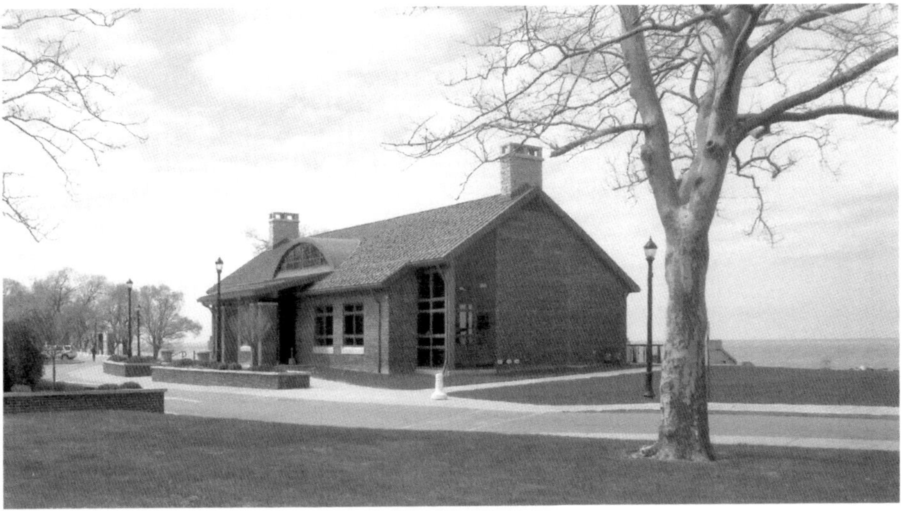

The Lakeview bathhouse today. *Courtesy of Robert T. Smith, Elyria, Ohio.*

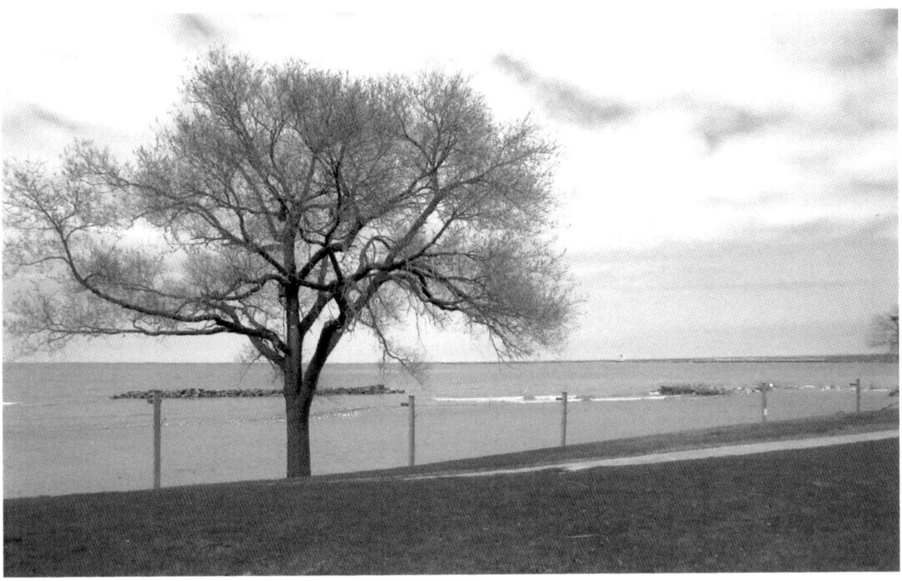

Lake Erie at Lakeview Park today. *Courtesy of Robert T. Smith, Elyria, Ohio.*

are in full bloom. You can walk along the paths and see the lake before you and, to the right, the famous Lorain lighthouse out on the peninsula.

Ninety years have come and gone, and the world has changed in remarkable ways. Moving along with the times, Lorain and Sandusky

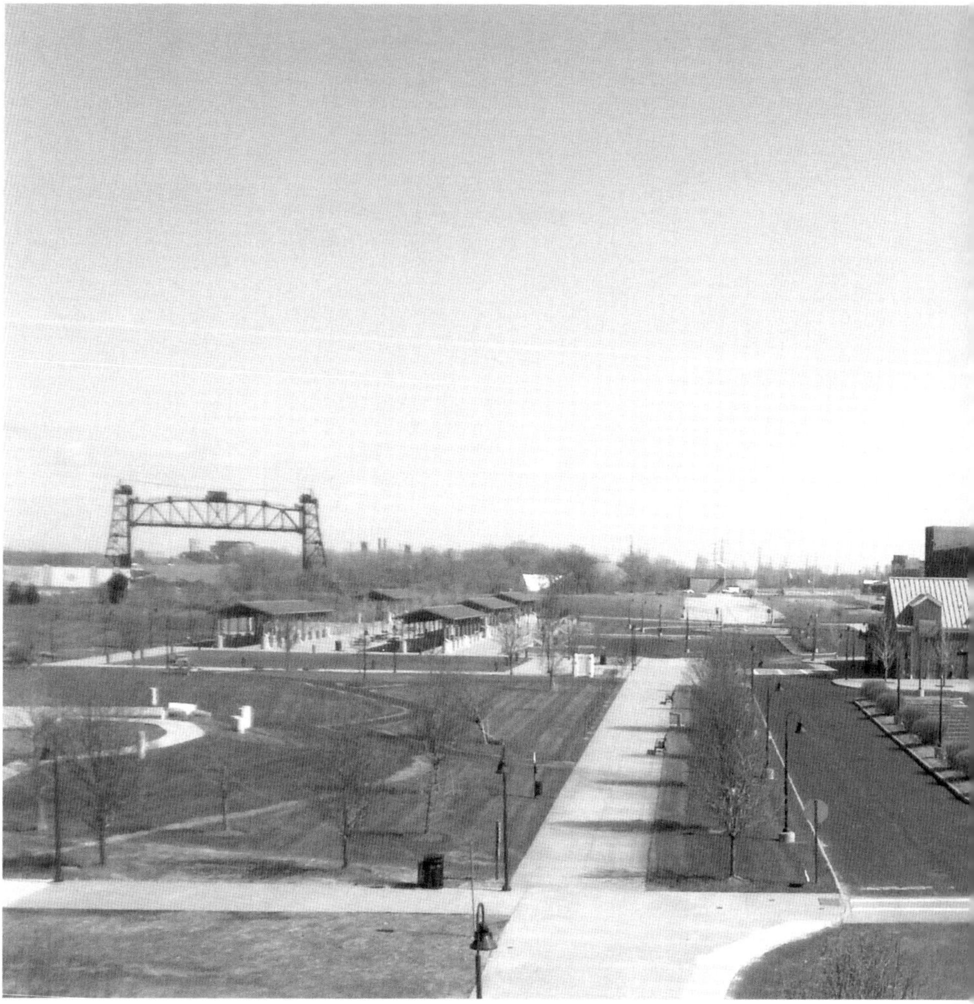

Black River Landing parking and information area. Built originally on the debris from the tornado, it is a vital part of the tourist industry today. *Courtesy of Robert T. Smith, Elyria, Ohio.*

are both thriving communities enjoying the benefits of living on the south shore of Lake Erie. There have been challenges: the closing of the steel plants, an uncertain economy and the poverty that comes with unemployment.

In 1967, American Shipbuilding would merge with Kinsman Marine Transit, owned by the Steinbrenner family, another north shore Ohio family. In that same year, George Steinbrenner, famed owner of the New York

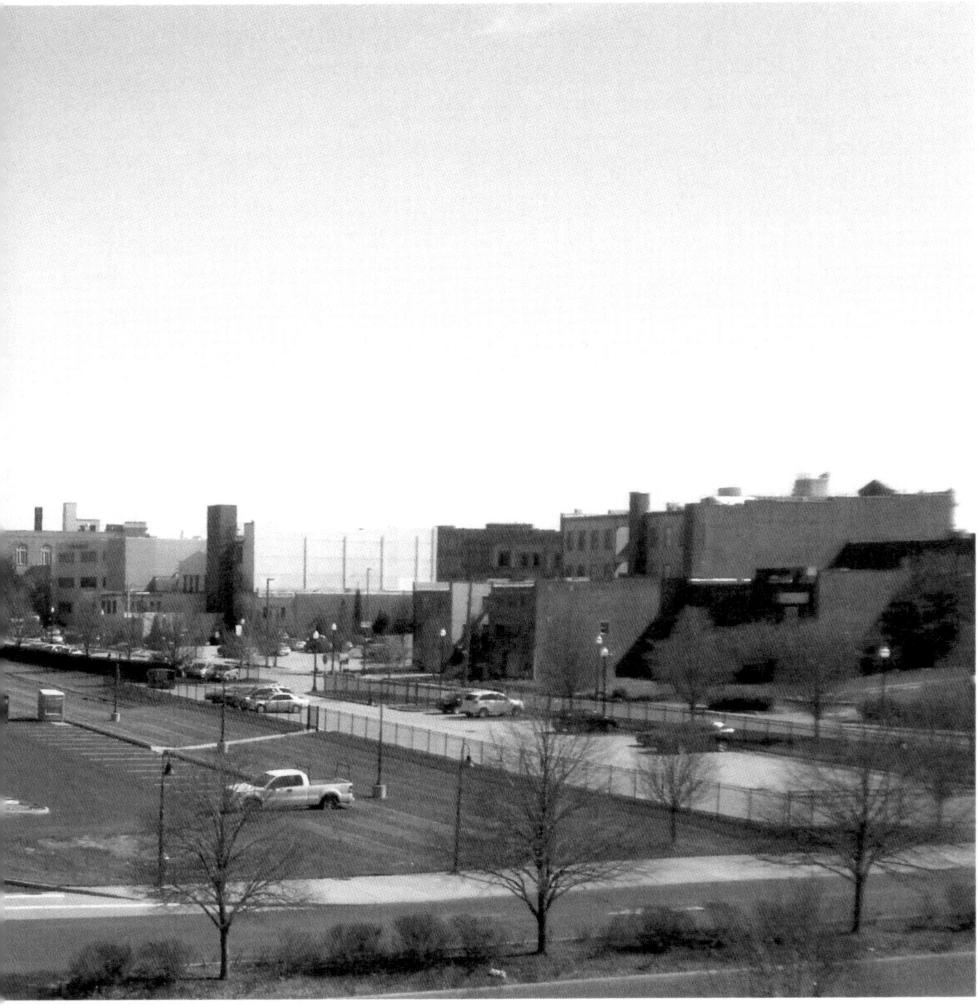

Yankees, would take the helm of the American Shipbuilding Company. In the 1980s, the American Shipbuilding Company closed its yards. George Steinbrenner died in 2010.

But along with these problems, the hardy people of Sandusky and Lorain moved on, changed their visions of the world and have survived. Over seventy different nationalities now live in Lorain or the surrounding area.

Today, the town of Sandusky is a thriving tourist destination on the western shore of Lake Erie. There is no sign of the destruction from ninety years ago. It is only when one follows the markers to Historic Sandusky that the modern visitor gets a glimpse into the past and what the world was like in 1924. Historic Sandusky, where the tornado actually made landfall, is a quaint and lovely part of the town. Its hilly streets lead down to the picturesque waterfront, and it is easy to imagine the world as it was ninety years ago.

Nearby is Cedar Point.

Contained on 364 acres, Cedar Point has been proclaimed the "greatest amusement park in the world." Each year, more than three million tourists from all over the world visit to enjoy the seventy-two rides, including sixteen roller coasters. Cedar Point is the only place in the world that can boast four roller coasters taller than two hundred feet. It is also listed as the second-oldest amusement park in North America. Visitors also swim and sunbathe on the mile-long beach and enjoy two water parks: the outdoor park Soak City and the indoor park Castaway Bay. To accommodate the three million visitors who arrive each year to test their courage is a huge layout of motels, restaurants and tourist support shops, sprawling for miles from the Ohio turnpike to the lake.

Lorain has a strong historical movement focused on restoration and acknowledgement of the city's unique history in the development of the United States. In keeping with this vision, the debris from the tornado moved to the mouth of the Black River is the foundation for the Black River Landing, at 421 Black River Street, a popular scene for celebrations and town events.

Every summer, concerts, fireworks, boat tournaments and community events take place there. One of the great summer events held at Black River Landing is the International Festival. It draws tourists from all over Ohio. It is held near the Ferry Building, where fun-seekers can catch a ride to the islands or hop on a fast boat to Cleveland.

Final Note: Lake Erie

In closing, I must report on the Lake Erie monster. The last sighting of Bessie was in 2004, and most Ohioans think of her with affection. There is a beer named for her, and a reward has been posted for a definitive sighting, though no one has claimed it as of this time.

In Memoriam

LIST OF THE VICTIMS WHO PERISHED

Lorain Victims

Mrs. Harriet Adams, 63, Cleveland: Struck by falling building and killed

Harry Artin, 35, Opera House Block: Perished in the collapse of the Dinery

Edward Bauman, 26: Died of a shattered skull sheltering his fiancée, Miss Cliffe Warmser, and her niece

Mrs. Eunice Beam, 52, Punxsutawney, Pennsylvania: Died at the Lakeview Park bathhouse

Mrs. Blanche Berg, 33, 1119 Ninth Street: Perished in the collapse of her father's home

Mrs. Catherine Blinzley, 48, 225 Fourteenth Street: Perished at the Lakeview Park bathhouse

Joseph Blinzley, 50, 225 Fourteenth Street: Perished at the Lakeview Park bathhouse

Harold Bouse, 64, 1345 Second Street

Mrs. Martha Braun, 69, 527 Hamilton Avenue: Killed while trying to fix an awning on her home

Evelyn Brown, 11, 552 Fifth Street: Perished in the collapse of the State Theater

Harry Buttle, 35, 558 Brownell Avenue: Died from perforated lungs caused by injuries at the Lakeview Park bathhouse.

William Buttle, 15, 558 Brownell Avenue: Killed at the Lakeview Park beach

Mrs. Mary Campbell, 21, 308 Seventh Street: Crushed to death at Crystal Restaurant

George Copas, 20, Elyria: Killed when his ambulance caught fire
Robert Coulter, 6, 534 Hamilton Avenue
George Csillag Jr., 8, 909 Front Street
George Csillag Sr., 40, 909 Front Street
John Danyi, 32, 1646 East Twenty-ninth Street: Killed by a falling building
John Delesimanvioec, 12, 909 East Thirty-second Street
Mathilda Diedrich, 14 months, 1839 East Thirty-fourth Street
Joseph Dina, 2, 409 Delaware Avenue
Mrs. Gertrude Fisk, 65, 733 Georgia Avenue Died when her house collapsed on her
Louis Foisy, 49, 1045 G Street: Killed in the destruction of his home
Mrs. Margaret Frame, 83, Elyria
Everett Gant, 35, Webb City, Missouri
Joseph Garbo, 9, 311 Colorado Avenue
Mrs. Martha Guignette, 32, 411 Idaho Avenue: Bookkeeper killed at work in her office
George Hamilton, 51, Steubenville: Killed while driving his automobile
Evelyn Hemple, 14, 1185 Eighth Street: Killed by a falling building
Mrs. Elizabeth Horvath, 37, 1004 Colorado Avenue
Professor Jeffreys, 60, Oberlin: Killed at Lakeview Park beach
Clark Keiver, 65, 314 Florida Avenue: Watchman killed when winds swept him off a bridge
Stephen Koch, 37, 1630 East Thirty-first Street
Mary Kodelja, 16, 1709 East Thirty-third Street: Clerk at Lakeview Beach Park—drowned
Mrs. Anna Kroll, 70, 412 Delaware Avenue: Killed in her destroyed home
William Kroll, 10, 412, Delaware Avenue: Killed in his destroyed home
Dorothy Lalonde, 12, 627 Broadway: Died in the Crystal Restaurant
Harold Lawenstein, 7: Killed at Lakeview Park bathhouse
Karl Lemmerman, 39, Cleveland
Harold Lewenstein, 28, Jersey City, New Jersey: Sailor born in Sweden—killed at Lakeview Park
Mrs. Effie McDonald, 30, Cincinnati
Mrs. Ellen Meredith, 45, Swissvale, Pennsylvania: Died at Lakeview Park bathhouse
Joseph Michalik, 33, 1215 West Twenty-second Street: Died at the American Shipyard, crushed by a falling smokestack
Stanley Michurski, 25, G Street
Mrs. Gertrude Mills, 49 1030 Ninth Street: Crushed to death in the collapse of her feed store

Margaret Mogzis, 9, 401 West Twenty-first Street: Died in the State Theater
Florence Nickley, 6, 616 Colorado Avenue
John T. Nolan, 35, 1736 Oberlin Avenue: Fireman killed by a falling building
Willis Plunkett, 17, 1339 Second Street: Killed by a falling building
Audrey Pressick, 7, 113 Arizona Avenue: Died in the State Theater
Albert Rheinsberg, 27, West Erie and Brownell Avenue: Killed in his automobile on Broadway
Mrs. Pauline Rheinsberg, 32, West Erie and Brownell Avenue: Killed in her automobile on Broadway
Eileen Rhodes, 10, 433 Idaho Avenue: Killed in the collapse of her home
Mrs. Grace Richards, 38, Columbus, Ohio: Died in the Van Deusen residence
Leonard Richards, 5, Columbus, Ohio: Died in the Van Deusen residence
Lois Richards, 3, Columbus, Ohio: Died in the Van Deusen residence
Ray Richards, 41, Columbus, Ohio: Died in the Van Deusen residence
John Shauver, 54, 319 Washington Avenue: Hurled to his death from a bridge
Florence Sheppard, 30, 1010 Ninth Street: Teacher who took refuge in the Colman Burnett Store and was killed when it collapsed
Mrs. Carrie Smith, 45, Opera House block: Killed in the Dinery
Mrs. Katie Spekhart, 65, 1117 G Street
Mrs. Mable Stickrath, 35, 841 G Street
Charles Stumpp, 28, Vermillion: Killed in his automobile when it was hit by flying debris
Wilbur Van Deusen, 3, 1128 Fifth Street: Died in the basement of the family home
Steve Vedro, 3219 Camden Avenue
Bessie Widzer, 12, 1326 Reid Avenue: Died in the State Theater
Stanley Williams, 34, 1133 Sixth Street
Mrs. Mary Witter, 57, 1032 Fifth Street: Succumbed to shock upon viewing the destruction
Carlton Woods, 12, 126 East Thirty-first Street: Died in the State Theater
Edward Wyttenbach, 28, Henrietta: Died at Lakeview Park or the Crystal Restaurant

Sandusky Victims

William Hampton, truck driver
John Hinton

Minetta Margard, bookkeeper
R.F. McKee, B&O freight engineer
Jake Schaefer, B&O watchman
Howard Vanbiarcum
Howard Wobser

Portage County Victims

Stanley Ferry, farmer
William Herbert, farmer
Henry Lorenz, farmer

In Memoriam

To those who died in the storm and were not recorded,
their identities known only to God.

BIBLIOGRAPHY

Documentaries

Koba & Company. *One Saturday Afternoon*. 1924.

Books, Newspapers and Magazines

American Insurance Digest and Insurance Manual, March 21, 1925.

Chronicle Telegram, June 29, 20, 1924; July 1, 2, 3, 4, 1924.

Cleveland Memory Project. Reminiscences of Esther Smallwood, n.d.

Cleveland Plain Dealer, June 29, 30, 1924; July 1, 2, 3, 1924.

Hoffman, George. *The Official Souvenir and Memorial Book of the Lorain Tornado, 1924*. N.p., n.d.

Lorain Times Herald, June 29, 30, 1924; July 1, 2, 3, 1924.

National Geographic 224, no. 5 (November 2013).

Red Cross Courier. Weekly Red Cross newsletter, July 1924.

Sandusky Register, June 29, 30, 1924; July 1, 2, 3, 4, 1924.

Online Data

Ancestry.com. www.ancestry.com.

Cleveland State University. Cleveland Memory Project. www.clevelandstate.org.

BIBLIOGRAPHY

Find a Grave. www.findagrave.com.

History of Lorain. www.lorainpubliclibrary.org.

Hunter, Herbert. "The Lorain, Ohio Tornado, June 28, 1924." Weather Bureau Report, Washington, D.C., n.d.

Ohio Historical Society. Ohio Memory Project. www.OHS.org.

Ohio Pix. www.OHS.org.

U.S. Department of Agriculture. Weather Bureau Climatological Data, Ohio. Section 6, Volume 29. July 1924.

Wikipedia. "Sandusky, Ohio." http://en.Wikipedia.org.

———. "Shipwrecks and Maritime Tales." www.wikipedia.com.

ABOUT THE AUTHOR

Betsy D'Annibale was born in Elyria, Ohio, and moved to New York State when she was ten. She is a graduate of Skidmore College, where she earned a bachelor of arts degree in European history and did graduate work in European history at the State University of New York at Albany. She has been a freelance writer for over thirty years and is the published author of two fiction novels and an assortment of nonfiction magazine and newspaper articles. *The 1924 Tornado in Lorain and Sandusky* is her most recent work.